Writing the Journeys We Never Wanted to Make

A Guide to Journalling for Resilience

Julia D McGuinness

Writing the Journeys We Never Wanted to Make

WELLNESS BOOKS

Copyright

Writing the Journeys We Never Wanted to Make
Copyright© 2025 Julia D McGuinness. All rights reserved.

No part of this publication may be reproduced, stored in a retrieval system, or transmitted in any form or by any means—electronic, mechanical, photocopying, recording, or otherwise without the prior written permission of the copyright holders.

Published in the United Kingdom by Wellness Books
www.wellnessbooks.co.uk

Portions of this book include previously published material, used with permission. Excerpts used for commentary under fair use/fair dealing principles.

This book is for informational purposes only and is not intended as medical, psychological, or therapeutic advice. If you have concerns about your mental or physical health, please consult a qualified medical or mental health professional.

Cover design by Iain Hill of 1981D

ISBN: 978-1-0684581-0-1
First published 2025
Printed in the United Kingdom

For

Julie Wetherill, whose warmth, wisdom, kindness and good humour as a counselling supervisor for thirteen years helped me navigate many a difficult turn in my professional journey.

Contents

Preface
Chapter 1: Reacting   1
Chapter 2: Resisting   19
Chapter 3: Reckoning   39
Chapter 4: Re-orientating   59
Chapter 5: Resourcing   79
Chapter 6: Re-energising   97
Chapter 7: Resolving   117
Chapter 8: Reconstituting   137
Chapter 9: Relapsing   155
References   170

Preface

It was August 31st, 1997. On the 6am news, the death of Princess Diana was being announced. My husband Gordon and I were living in Nottingham, and going through the last phase of a fertility treatment we hoped would result in the children we had longed for over the previous twelve years. On the morning of that fateful car crash in the Paris tunnel, we were setting off for an early appointment at Nottingham's Queen's Medical Centre. I remember hearing the news as I got dressed, and abruptly sitting back down to take in what I – and many others that day – could scarcely believe had happened.

The following week, as I obeyed doctor's orders to rest as much as I could, I spent hours in front of the TV, watching the rising tide of floral tributes. Nothing felt real amid this outpouring of grief at a journey that had ended all too abruptly.

Our fertility treatment was unsuccessful, and somehow that week of mourning for the end of Diana's life became woven into a marking of sorrow at the end of our own hopes of having children. We had already decided that this venture would be our last throw of the fertility dice. It felt particularly poignant, as our wedding had been in the same month as Charles and Diana's — we had returned from our honeymoon to watch their rather more lavish nuptials.

Unexplained infertility was a journey I never expected, or wanted, to make. But, years later, I have come to a peace and different fulfilment of the parenting energy I have been given. A stack of black, hard-backed journals still stands at the back of my wardrobe, holding all the writing I did along the way. They remind me how life has moved me on to different journeys, and of how much putting my own words onto the page helped me then, as it continues to do.

Life, for all of us, involves the interplay between the journeys we want to make, and the ones we find imposed upon us. There is something of a paradox here, though: the journeys we do intend can involve unforeseen obstacles and implications, whilst those we never wanted may open out into a richness we could never have anticipated.

The death of my dream of biological parenthood proved to be as much the start of a journey as the end of one — as disorientating as for the travellers in the poet T S Eliot's *Journey of the Magi*, where the Speaker wonders whether the outcome of his travels was to witness a birth or experience a death; he concludes that, somehow, it was both.

I had never imagined twelve years earlier that I would be in this position. Having been blessed with a secure upbringing, good health, a stimulating education through to university and subsequent teaching post as an English teacher at a boys' grammar school — getting married along the way — I had no reason to suspect that life would not continue as before.

The unspoken assumption of my husband and myself, amid a society so insistent on the importance of contraception, was that as soon as we threw caution to the winds, we would find ourselves in the family way. It was not to be, and we were ill-prepared for what followed, in all its disappointment, confusion, frustration and sorrow; not to mention uncertainty, questions and a sense of exile.

It is many years since those painful days, and I now look back from a very different place. There have been more unwanted journeys since, but as a more seasoned traveller, I have learnt to manage them better. I have become more aware of what such journeys entail and, in particular, of how helpful the writing process can be in maintaining both equilibrium and momentum along the path. Although I wrote through those earlier dark times, I wish I had known the range of possibilities of how I could use writing for support in what was happening with me at different points.

I have begun with my personal experience of infertility but, however different the circumstances, we all find ourselves on roads we never chose to travel, at times. The starting point of an unwanted personal journey is likely to involve a significant loss of some kind: of person, relationship, job, health, dream, youth, capacity, future, perhaps home. When I mentioned my book title to a workshop group, someone said: '"Unwanted Journeys"? That's just about life, then, isn't it?' There was immediate assent all round the room.

Finding ourselves in an unfamiliar place when life has suddenly pitched us off the road can evoke in us a desire to pick up a pen, to find words for what is happening, to help us navigate our way through.

Our relationship with writing may vary. Some of us have a natural tendency to write and may already be writing regularly. Some may have always wanted to write and their new situation fuels that desire, providing the opportunity of unexpected time they never previously had. Others may be less comfortable with writing — perhaps a legacy of school-day experiences — but feel it could be useful if only they had more confidence. Some have spent a career writing technical reports rather than personal material. Others want to find a way to help themselves rather than over-rely on family, friends or counselling support.

However we come to it, writing to support our well-being has plenty to offer, as we explore its potential. Writing our unwanted journeys may help us to:

- Validate experience
- Ground ourselves
- Express feelings
- Affirm identity
- Clarify confusion
- Preserve memories
- Track progress
- Gain insight
- Explore creativity
- Solve problems

The experience of an unwanted journey takes us through a series of different processes.

Each of the eight processes, as I have observed them, forms the theme of a chapter in this book. Every chapter comprises a reflection on the process and the territory it occupies in the loss landscape, some personal experiences of myself and others, and suggestions for your own writing in the form of journalling activities and responses to poetry.

Journalling can help us keep track of how we are travelling. The journalling suggestions in each chapter draw on different approaches; they are intended to be particularly applicable to the process being explored, but you can of course transpose them to other aspects of your journey as you wish. As you go through the book, you will build up a repertoire of journalling tools for you to deploy as needed.

Poetry is a writing form people can find themselves naturally turning to during times of heightened emotion and crisis; it offers an appropriate container for the intensity of feeling and possibilities of insight. The language of poetry moves us out of the headspace of rational analysis, down to where the heart and the spirit take the lead. It does not insist on having everything tidily resolved but is a companion that will travel with us to the edge of our comfort zone and help us find words for what is beyond. The poems in each chapter may simply be read and reflected on but you are also invited to explore their promptings yourself in a writing activity.

I have arranged the processes we go through in our unwanted journeys in the order in which they are likely to be experienced. Unwanted journeys, however, rarely follow a neat and predictable sequence; they unfold in their own way and time, involving detours, back-trackings and repetitions. You may wish to adopt this more flexible approach while reading this book.

Life's unwanted journeys come in many permutations, with many different pathways to becoming a member of what I call 'The Loss Club'. My hope is that as you read and write your way through the terrain, you will reach what one workshop participant described as 'The Found Club', which lies just beyond the horizon.

Chapter 1: Reacting

- Not engaging with a situation
- Out of touch with emotion
- Articulating only surface facts
- Keeping things unconscious
- Limited in capacity to absorb
- Overwhelmed by circumstances
- Aware of vulnerability
- Operating as normal or at a standstill

'You're blasted off in a rocket, and then suddenly you find you've crash landed on Planet Cancer', was how one patient described to me her experience of diagnosis. In the space of a day, she felt catapulted into a whole new, alien world.

I will never forget myself and my husband's initial visit to the GP for a fertility clinic referral — a situation I never saw coming. And in recent years, a phone call from another GP to discuss the results of my knee X-Rays: 'Your joints are shot,' he announced. 'You're not far off full replacement surgery.'

We do not choose to embark on such journeys. We are not heroes answering a higher call; rather, we become exiles, jolted out of the world we thought we knew by an unwelcome life event we cannot fix and for which we have no map.

Desired journeys start with a dream: a challenge leading towards an envisioned reward. Unwanted journeys start with a loss — of a relationship or loved one, health or capacity, location or home, job or role — and we can feel propelled into a nightmare.

Perhaps you can remember the day such a seismic shift cut the ground from under your feet. It was a day of bad news: the day of failed test results; the day your burntout body and soul finally refused to get up for work; the day of a redundancy notice; when a loved-one breathed their last; when the accident happened; the day home was no longer home; or when a pandemic locked you down. The familiar landscape has gone; the unthinkable has actually taken place, pitching you into a wilderness way beyond your comfort zone.

When such shifts in our lives threaten to overwhelm us, our internal defence systems kick in, as they attempt to protect us. We may find ourselves numbed into a state of shock, paralysed and unable to act or make any decision at all.

Or it may be that we disconnect from this life event's full implications and move into denial. We simply continue to function on automatic pilot. This is one reason why the bereaved sometimes seem to manage so well at a funeral; the momentous reality of what has happened has not fully hit, so they go on 'as normal'.

When my father was finally diagnosed with oesophageal cancer after a period of increasing difficulty in swallowing food, alongside other symptoms, my parents did not call to let me know. I had no inkling of this serious turn of events until I asked how things were going during my regular phone call to them. My father told me his diagnosis in a tone of voice that sounded as if he were describing a slightly unusual case of the flu. Whilst I was reeling, he seemed to be dismissing his condition as a bit of a nuisance, his words disconnected from their full significance. I now understand this not as a casual response, but as an unconscious realisation that it was all too much to take on board. Instinctively, he was keeping this news off his emotional radar. To let it in could be overwhelming. It had to be business as usual; it just had to be, didn't it?

In the process of reacting, we have no stomach for any sort of journeying. Our energy, such as it is, is deployed into avoidance, blocking any acknowledgement that a journey awaits at all. If we feel anything, it is a sense of ending rather than beginning.

We may have been hurled into this process through a traumatic event or loss that has come totally out of the blue; the ground has dropped from under our feet. Or we may have had an inkling of clouds gathering. Either way, we come to a tipping point that pitches us to the point of no return, short-circuiting our capacity to respond.

If part of us has been sensing a change in the air, it may only take a trivial incident to push us over the edge. Up to that point, we may have simply dismissed the appearance of unwelcome cracks by unconsciously redoubling our efforts to keep going. Yet, the more capably we have done this, the greater the final crisis. After being at full stretch to keep the show on the road, the inevitable fall is harder; our own strengths have been working against us. Reacting can seem like an absence of process, a place of numbness and disconnection. It is more a state of shock absorption. Behind the scenes, our system is taking the time it needs to readjust to a world upturned or shattered into pieces.

Each process on the unwanted journey has its natural rhythm. Being in this place may be necessary for a season but it is not our forever home. We need the kind arms of some time to steady us; some warmth for our frozenness and some gentle ways to start to engage with our newly alien surroundings.

Why Write?

If you are in a process where it is difficult even to say what is going on for you, you may be wondering why it might help to write about these things at all. Can writing really do us good?

The answer is that many have instinctively found that it does. Their discoveries are backed up by evidence emerging from a stream of research into the therapeutic benefits of expressive writing, pioneered in the 1980s by James Pennebaker, Professor Emeritus of Psychology at the University of Austin in Texas. Pennebaker was particularly interested in the impact of writing about difficult personal experiences that had never been disclosed. His original experiment involved two groups of students, both instructed to write freely for a daily, timed period of 15-20 minutes over several consecutive days. One group was asked to write about deeply traumatic events, perhaps those about which they had never spoken; the other group was simply to write about everyday events.

Although the trauma-writing students felt more emotional during, and in the immediate aftermath of, writing, this tended to subside. After a few months, Pennebaker discovered that these students made half the number of visits to the health centre, recording lower blood pressure and better overall health than the everyday-writing students. In subsequent years, nearly 200 further research studies have been undertaken, with outcomes confirming the benefits of moving our internal distress outwards by writing it down. As well as improving psychological and emotional well-being, this can enable the body to heal more efficiently. Disclosure to the safe space of a page brings release. What is now known as the Pennebaker method has become a model for using personal and expressive writing in a beneficial way. Four key elements contribute to making this writing fruitful:

- Write honestly and deeply about what troubles you
- Set a time-limit on this writing
- Re-read the writing and reflect on what you notice about it
- Do something with these reflections. What do you want to take away from this writing session?

These steps can help you pace and protect your ventures into troubled territory. Personal writing can stir some deep emotional waters but we want it to move us onward to a better place, not to entrench us in the mire.

Although it may feel risky to pick up the pen, Pennebaker's research indicates that not disclosing a traumatic experience in some way may harbour its own risks. One experiment involved 100 senior engineers made redundant without prior warning. Those who wrote about this traumatic experience were more successful in securing new jobs than those who did not. Disclosing their anger around the shock of abrupt redundancy enabled the trauma-writers to release and process their feelings; they were not carrying unresolved emotional baggage into future job interviews.

James Pennebaker's research highlights that its therapeutic benefits may be one reason to write, but what does writing mean to you? Whether you are drawn to write for the first time, or are a regular writer, it can be helpful to clarify why you want to do it. This can bring some focus and momentum to your writing process. Perhaps you are on a difficult journey — a season of some sort of loss — and want to write to help yourself through.

Some other reasons you might want to write could include:

- Talking to the page as a companion when you are alone
- Tracking life lived with more intention

- Finding a place to order, focus and prioritise
- Making decisions
- Processing feelings
- Celebrating the positives, to encourage a healthy perspective
- Expressing gratitude
- Savouring memories
- Managing yourself and your life

Perhaps it is hard to identify exactly why you want to write; you just know that you do. A friend whose brother and hill-climbing companion died prematurely found a keen desire to write surfacing on its own. He was not sure why, but he knew he wanted to write something personal and different from the formal, professional writing he was used to producing. He started by recording the details of the hill-climbs he and his brother had made together, as a way of registering them for posterity and for the wider family to share. He ordered the events of his brother's life into a biographical list. He wrote about the profound moments at his brother's bedside in those final hours. He wrote to explore his own reflections on life's journey, its meaning and his faith.

So, why do you want to write? Use the Pennebaker method outlined above, writing honestly, within a chosen time-limit and re-reading your writing reflectively. Start with the words 'I want to write because…' and keep writing whatever comes up. There is no right or wrong in what you put down on the page, and you do not have to conclude with a clear-cut answer. Allow exploring the question to be enough.

If you find yourself conflicted about the writing process, try the same exercise with the opening words, 'I don't want to write, because…', and see what that may reveal. There can be a variety of reasons underlying resistance to writing: anxiety about what it may bring up; having to get the writing 'right'; memories of a bad experience of writing at school; worry about who might get to read it. But once you have identified the resistance, you may be able to see ways of overcoming it.

So why do *you* want to write?

Emilie's Story: Writing to Heal

A difficult life event became the catalyst for Emilie picking up her pen to face and deal with a painful family history.

Emilie was in her 30s when her terminally-ill mother left Emilie's abusive father after a 35-year destructive marriage. Emilie had long seen this coming, but, she explained, 'When the tragic climax arrived, I knew I needed to write the story I had always carried, and to get it out of my system.'

Growing up, Emilie kept diaries and wrote letters. She had more than 50 childhood penpals. Now, she sensed that her writing could be a healing tool to help her to make sense of her changing world. Emilie was unsure where to start, so began with some gentle, free-writing about her father's past, seeking insight into 'where his darkness stemmed from'. She experimented with different approaches, writing through the eyes of her father, grandmother and mother, as well as her own; and explored questions about her father's upbringing, and what his own mother (her grandmother) had been like in those early years. Emilie's safe writing space was her home office, but she also made notes when out and about — on the train or in a café. She wrote daily and, at times, very intensively.

Writing helped Emilie let go of long-standing resentments and move towards acceptance and forgiveness. Telling her family's story from other perspectives deepened her understanding of the bigger picture, and how a story can have many facets and layers. Emilie's writing journey led to a calling to help others find ways of writing to heal their own stories. She no longer felt powerless and weighed down by shame, and even adapted her story into a script to send out to a publisher.

It was rejected, but though initially devastated, Emilie realised that, ultimately, it was the writing, not publication, that mattered: 'The searching and the emotions that I tackled and overcame in the writing process are my greatest gift, as I teach writing for healing.' Writing 'has changed how I view relationships with other people, made me reassess my life, shifted my priorities, lowered my tolerance towards poorer relationships, widened my perspective and deepened my understanding', says Emilie.

She advises that when writing about distressing experiences, plenty of reflection time is needed, both before and afterwards: 'Self-care is very important. We can't rush this process, however urgent it feels. By going gently, we gradually get more access to our stories, and ourselves.

'Your writing will surprise you; it might be a completely different story from the one you planned, but stay open-minded and curious, and let your writing go where it needs to. Allow yourself to feel everything, then you can gradually let go and allow healing to begin.'

Emilie reflected in her journal:

'By daring to follow my pen and unveil the places where the sting was sharpest, I changed and found unexpected courage. By exploring the core of the trauma of my family of origin, I could see patterns with unexpected clarity and draw parallels. It gave me a new direction and the courage to move back to my native Sweden and found a course in "Healing Writing"; a course I wished I'd had the opportunity to take myself when I was in need. The circle was thus closed in an unexpected and powerful way.'

In the Reacting process, writing may help you to:

- Stay connected to the world around you
- Set intentions to find a focus
- Locate a safe place to nurture yourself
- Pay attention to your welfare
- Take on gently what you can manage
- Steady yourself exactly where you are
- Shelter and nurture yourself
- Acknowledge a starting point

Journalling Suggestions

> Stay connected to the world around you

Sensory Check-in

When we feel as if we are cut off from the world and living in a small, separate bubble of our own, simply bringing our attention to our senses can be a gentle way of tuning into the world around us. Try noting down the following:

- Something I can see now
- The first sound I heard this morning
- A taste that can bring me pleasure
- The last thing I remember touching
- The smell of the air around me as I breathe in

Any of these can be a springboard for writing a little more, if you wish.

You could choose one sensory stimulus to expand on in a few short sentences; perhaps it has made a particular impression on you or evokes some strong associations. As an alternative, you could start by choosing one sense and writing down the different things it has brought to your awareness over the day.

Afterwards, add a sentence or two reflecting on what you notice from your writing, and how you feel now. It does not have to be an earth-shattering revelation! You might just observe that you feel calmer after taking some moments to re-connect to your senses and put some words down for what is around you right now.

You could make this a regular practice for a few minutes each day for a while.

> Set intentions to find focus

Sentence Stems

At times, we may disconnect from our emotions for self-protection. This can make it hard to generate the energy to move out into the life of the day. Finding a few words to complete a single sentence is an immediate way of finding a focus on something specific — an action we can take; an encouragement that grounds us. It can spark the energy to bring something in us to life. Try completing the sentence stems below:

The most important thing to do today is...

Today I will...

Today I will not...

Something I can do now that I'll be glad I've done is...

One good thing about today is...

What is helping me most at the moment is...

What I need most at the moment is...

One small step I can take right now is...

You can work through all of these.

You might want to add some new sentence stems of your own. You could also take one or two and complete them several times, either at one sitting or daily; if you do this, it can be interesting to note if, and how, your sentence endings change.

> Locate a safe place to nurture yourself

A Safe Space

If we are embarking on a difficult journey and feeling vulnerable, we need to feel as supported as possible. Where is the safe space that you can return to, to recuperate, rest, recover and be relaxed? Where can you be your 'shoes-off self'?

Take a few deep breaths and close your eyes. Let yourself picture the safest space you could ever find yourself in. What emerges for you? You may wish to find a blank sheet of paper and sketch out your safe space. It may be a real place, an imagined place or a place where you have always longed to go.

Now, imagine you are in front of a door. This is the door that leads to your safest space in the world, and you are holding the key. Write about what the door looks like and how this key feels in your hand. Write about opening the door. How does it feel? Does the key turn and the door open easily? Do you lock it behind you?

Write about what you see as you step through the open door. Use all your senses to describe this place. What can you see, hear, touch, smell, taste? How do you feel? What makes this space so attractive to you?

Take time to describe it in as much detail as possible and settle yourself there. Afterwards, reflect on how writing about this space has made you feel. Remember, you have the key. You can return in your imagination at any time.

> Pay attention to your welfare

Sustenance Template

If we want to use writing to help us but do not know where to start, a structured journalling approach is a useful way in. This may especially be so at times when our energy is low, or we fear what might appear on the page if we just start writing.

When events have left us fragile, our immediate need is to undergird our well-being with some self-care; this will strengthen our capacity to navigate our way through difficult territory on the page when we are ready.

Template journalling is one approach that can help if we are daunted by the blank page. A template is a set format of particular prompts, with space left for us to fill in our response to each one in just a sentence or two. It offers a clear, set structure that we can repeat as often as we choose. Containing our writing in this way protects us from becoming stuck or over-burdened.

Below are some suggested headings for a 'Sustenance Template'. Take each heading and write your own response underneath. Repeat over successive days/weeks, as needed. Repeating it will start attuning you to notice what the template asks you to write about.

You can also adjust these headings or replace them to create a template of your own.

Sustenance Template

Something sensory that has engaged my attention today (e.g., a piece of music, food, a particular sight, touch or smell)

....

A positive emotion I felt today — even fleetingly — and what prompted it

....

I acknowledge one unwelcome emotion or thought today

....

Where has kindness been in my life today (given or received, or maybe in a way I've been kind to myself)?
....

One way I have cared for my body today (rest, exercise, good nutrition, etc.)
....

Someone or something living (pet, plant, etc.) I have connected with positively in some way today
....

Something I'm glad I have done today
....

One thing I can do tomorrow to look after myself
....

Poetry Exploration

> Take on gently what you can manage

Don't give me the whole truth

Don't give me the whole truth,
don't give me the sea for my thirst,
don't give me the sky when I ask for light,
but give me a glint, a dewy wisp, a mote
as the birds bear water-drops from their bathing
and the wind a grain of salt.

Olav H. Hauge

When everything seems overwhelming, we need to pace ourselves so as not to be overloaded beyond our capacity. The above poem, translated from Norwegian, speaks to this. In its first three lines, the Speaker refuses the overwhelming gifts of whole truth, sea and sky. Can you think of any parallel images from the natural world or even man-made environment that would reflect this sense of too much coming at you?

The poem then moves to related, smaller-scale gifts that are more easily received and absorbed. Can you find your own equivalents from the images you conjured as examples, that are enough for the moment? Set these out in a list of a line or two.

The poem's simple beauty conveys the idea that we may only be able to take on so much at a time, especially if we are feeling fragile. Think about your own situation now, or at times when you have felt vulnerable to overload. At such times, less can be more.

On the left side of the page, list the good things that could be too much of a good thing. Opposite, write the level at which that good thing could benefit you in your current state, e.g.:

a large chocolate cake…….. a slice of cake; an afternoon in deep conversation….. a ten-minute catch-up with a friend.

You might want to re-arrange these as a *list poem*. A list poem presents its content as a line by line inventory. It does not have to rhyme, but it is not random. We can make creative choices in how we order its elements.

Could you find a way to regulate some of these good things so you can engage with them at a level that is supportive rather than draining?

> Steady yourself as and where you are

Trough

There is a trough in waves,
a low spot
where horizon disappears
and only sky
and water
are our company.

And there we lose our way
unless
we rest, knowing the wave will bring us
to its crest again.

There we may drown
if we let fear

hold us in its grip and shake us
side to side,
and leave us flailing, torn, disoriented.

But if we rest there
in the trough,
in silence,
being with
the low part of the wave,
keeping
our energy and
noticing the shape of things,
the flow,
then time alone
will bring us to another
place
where we can see
horizon, see the land again,
regain our sense
of where
we are,
and where we need to swim.

Judy Brown

Being out of our depth and lost at sea can stir fears in any of us. This poem focusses on the image of the deep trough of water between the passing of mighty waves. It is a vulnerable place that threatens our survival, evoking feelings of powerlessness and panic in its absence of landmarks.

The poem urges a counter-intuitive approach: to rest into this void of uncertainty and loss of control, rather than try to pull out of it; to trust natural momentum to carry us forward, so that in due course we will see 'where we need to swim'. The poem's single-sentence stanza in a shape-shifting flow of free verse reflects its content.

Read the poem slowly, breathing in its words and savouring the surrounding space. You may want to speak it aloud, softly. Which phrases resonate most?

Amidst whatever waves dominate your particular horizon, try shifting your attention to write about the 'shape of things' around you: key moments of your day, those you meet, what you do, what you notice. You may want to write simply, briefly, and in fragments — perhaps following the poem's free verse pattern.

Such writing may help you steady your connection to life so you are cradled in the immediacy of the present moment. *Trough* suggests questions for its reader; you might like to write your response to such questions as:

- What does it mean for you to 'rest' in this space?
- How can you ensure you are keeping your energy?
- What adjustments might you make to enable these?

> Shelter and nurture yourself

The Me Before

Please don't be kind to me
Don't make eye contact
Or look at me that way
Save your pity for others
Then I'll be okay

Please don't be kind to me
Hold a blank expression
That offers no compassion
Like it's not important to you
Who I am

Please don't be kind to me
Don't touch my arm
Or walk by my side
Stay ahead and detached
Like there's nothing to hide

Please don't be kind to me
Show me the room

Like I'm not staying long
With an air of indifference
And then I'll be strong

Please don't be kind to me
Close the file on me now
Like I'm the me
I was
Before
Please don't be kind to me

Sharron Green

When times are tough, we can feel fragile. Instinctively, we may draw back from the expressions of kindness that threaten to expose us.

In this poem of stark, unpunctuated requests, do you identify with the Speaker's insistence that others keep their distance, both emotionally and physically? Have there been times when you have wanted to say these things?

This approach may keep us intact for a while, but eventually our emotions break cover, sometimes in response to that faithful friend who persists through our protestations; sometimes, seemingly out of the blue at the most inappropriate moment. But this can be a blessing in disguise. We need to be real to be healed.

Writing offers a safe space to acknowledge, at our own pace, what we are hiding. The page is always detached, and does not judge or intrude.

Choose a situation where you feel vulnerable and seek to hold people at bay. Write about how you imagine you might respond if someone was kind to you. As you find words for these fears, press further into this by answering a second question: if what you are fearing here did actually come to pass, what about that would be difficult for you?

If it is hard to receive kindness just now, are there some gentle ways you can find to be kind to yourself? Note down one or two things you can do to look after yourself, and determine to put them into practice.

The Me Before is a complete injunction against any gesture of kindness. When the chips are down, things can seem very all or nothing; but the way forward may be more nuanced.

Write about where you desire distance, and where — or from whom — you might risk receiving kindness. In some situations, being left to function as normal is appropriately sheltering. But alongside this, we need those one or two people to whom we can open up for deeper support — those whom we trust will indeed 'close the file' on who we were, but only in order to meet us fully as we are now.

> Acknowledge a starting point

On the Other Side

Through the looking glass,
down the rabbit hole,
into the wardrobe and out
into the enchanted forest
where animals talk
and danger lurks and nothing
works quite the way it did before,
you have fallen into a new story.
It is possible that you
are much bigger — or smaller —
than you thought.
It is possible to drown
in the ocean of your own tears.
It is possible that mysterious friends
have armed you with magical weapons
you don't yet understand,
but which you will need
to save your own life and the world.
Everything here is foreign.
Nothing quite makes sense.
That's how it works.
Do not confuse the beginning
of the story with the end.

Lynn Ungar

Chapter 1: Reacting

When something overturns our familiar world, we can feel that our future has been snatched away from us, though in truth none of us really knows what lies ahead.

In a nod to the popular children's stories, Lewis Carroll's *Alice in Wonderland* and the magic of C. S. Lewis' 'Narnia', the poet highlights how, from rabbit-hole to wardrobe, the ordinary can become a portal into an unfamiliar world where none of the old rules apply. The only certainty is uncertainty, alongside a plethora of possibilities and impossibilities. Yet, the Speaker reassures us that what feels strange is actually the norm here, and that what feels like an ending may actually be the start of a new adventure.

When I read this poem with a group, one participant resonated immediately with the situation. She recalled how a significant accident had once landed her in hospital, upending her life.

A poem can bring the consolation that our predicament is not unique, as it locates us on the map of human experience. We may face many sudden changes — an unexpected loss, a diagnosis, accident to self or a loved one, leaving a job without another one to go to, moving area, etc.

Write about a time past, when you found yourself suddenly in an unfamiliar situation, perhaps one you chose — such as a new job or area — or one you were thrust into.

Which phrases in the poem re-connect you to what you went through?

In what ways do you now see that time as a beginning rather than an ending?

To what extent does this alter your feelings and thoughts about that situation?

What letter would you write from yourself today to your past self, as an encouragement to see that situation as a beginning not an ending?

Writing about the past offers distance and objectivity, as we are beyond the emotional immediacy of it all. If you feel able, you may wish to write about any current circumstances of upheaval.

Are you feeling 'bigger — or smaller' than before?

What is not working or making sense at the moment?

What feels foreign or dangerous?

Where might possibilities lie?

Take this writing gently and do not press too far out of your comfort zone. This exercise is about expressing something of where you are, without having to resolve or understand it.

When you find yourself…	Writing may help you to…
• Not engaging with a situation	• Stay connected to the world around you
• Out of touch with emotion	• Set intentions to find a focus
• Articulating only surface facts	• Locate a safe place to nurture yourself
• Keeping things unconscious	• Pay attention to your welfare
• Limited in capacity to absorb	• Take on gently what you can manage
• Overwhelmed by circumstances	• Steady yourself as, and where, you are
• Aware of vulnerability	• Shelter and nurture yourself
• Operating as normal or ground to a halt	• Acknowledge a staring point

Chapter 2: Resisting

- Persisting with old strategies
- Angry at self/others/situation
- Pushing away voices that echo the truth
- Fighting emotional battles
- Feeling defensive
- Refusing to consider other outcomes
- Feeling unjustly done by
- Looking for magical solutions

I feel something of it right now as I sit down to write this chapter: resistance. I will look anywhere but the computer screen. I am suddenly stirred by a kitten fight on the rug; the itch to check social media; the urgency of the pile of clothes waiting to go into the washing machine. It all expresses my deliberate resistance to what I know very well is underneath: the fear of getting down to writing and maybe finding I cannot do it.

These symptoms occur with a journey I have *chosen* to be on — that of writing this book. But what about the journeys I have not wanted to make? I am aware of two particular unwanted personal journeys that have both involved the process of resistance.

With infertility, resistance came in the rhythm of my repeated re-framing of the timing of pregnancy. With each passing month of dashed hopes, I simply re-configured the dates; next month would be different. I re-calculated the optimum days for conception alongside a new projected date for leaving my teaching job, just adding on that one extra term. I justified why things had not worked out this time round: I had been particularly stressed; needed to drink less, pray more. I researched and read about couples who had conceived after a long wait, comforting myself that at least we were not as badly off as them.

As we started with investigations and treatment, disappointment gave way to stubborn determination. We *would* find a way through this — success in fixing the problem was just around the corner. My ruthless positivity was a weapon against the unthinkable.

Decades later, osteoarthritis made its presence known in my knee joints. I had taken up mid-life running and was having trouble trying to get back on track after a third half-marathon, which in itself had felt so much more of a slog than my excited first finish just a year or two earlier. Now, I could only jog for a few scant minutes before having to drop back to a walking pace.

The GP manipulated my painful joints. 'I think there's a touch of arthritis, there,' she said. I dismissed it. To me, arthritis was just an old folks' grumble. I was surprised to hear the word and internally disputed the diagnosis; this was surely just a bit of minor stiffness that would get better. I tried resting. Things did not improve.

Meanwhile, my mother's Parkinson's Disease was worsening and her health declining, as dementia began to take hold. My attention was claimed by another undesired journey. Six months later, some weeks after her funeral, I began to register just how continuously sore and awkward my knees felt. Wise advice came from a chance conversation with an older arthritis sufferer: 'Get it checked out,' she said. 'I ignored my symptoms and soldiered on. Then one day, I couldn't get out of bed.'

With some trepidation, I went to my GP, requested an X-ray and faced a diagnosis of advanced knee osteoarthritis. My head at last began to grapple with the facts, even though my heart was still busily intent on pushing this reality away.

Resisting what we know to be true but do not want to take on board emerges in many forms. For me, it was a deliberate blanking of increasing evidence to the contrary; an insistent positive thinking that things would all work out. I just needed to persist long enough to find a fix, and life would go back to normal.

When we deny something, our reactive aversion buries the unthinkable deep down. It may drop so far out of sight that we are emotionally disconnected from it. We only actively resist what has surfaced into consciousness. All too aware of the disturbance, we kick back, in an effort to suppress the discomfort of what we know is breaking through. Our subconscious may temporarily succeed in keeping the unacceptable in the dark, but it cannot subdue its power. It is like trying to lock troublesome children in the basement; once out, they run riot. Similarly, the resisting process can find us in the grip of strong, sometimes wayward, feelings. This is the territory of an emotional Buckaroo, where a seemingly minor or unrelated pressure point can trigger an over-reaction that throws us off-balance, to the shock of those around us. Beyond the smiling numbness of denial, resisting can elicit strong feelings. Others' words can touch on a raw spot, either unintentionally or even spoken in a genuine desire to help.

When we are resisting, those around us sometimes cannot do right for doing wrong. If they act as though all is well, they are being dismissive; if they seek to come alongside, they are being intrusive and insensitive. We may become snappy, or stubborn; supreme in our confidence that all will be well, against a backdrop of contrary voices — including our own; angry at the injustice of our circumstances. And to cap it all, we can be inconsistent, our own responses varying from day to day.

The initial shock of infertility was the beginning of one unwanted journey for me, with the resisting process being part of it. A few years down the line, we made the decision to draw a line of resolution under the matter, after a final round of medical treatment — whatever the outcome. The treatment's failure took me spiralling back into the resisting process all over again, as I was faced with coming to terms with the finality of unexplained and permanent infertility.

I did not want to face it. I fought back against the engulfing emotions of despair. Armed with a bottle of red wine and the most enormous bar of chocolate I could find, I shut myself in the spare room with a huge jigsaw (Renoir's *The Boating Party*. At 4,500 pieces, I never completed it then and have not done since). I had withdrawn into my cave, intent on bolstering myself from pain and escaping as best I could from how life was hurting. Everything felt too raw to expose to the world outside.

It felt natural and necessary to take time out to recuperate, like an animal lying low to lick its wounds. But soon I realised that what I had fled to the cave to avoid was with me. Whilst I recoiled from facing others, I needed to face what was going on in myself.

Mythologist and writer Joseph Campbell observes: 'Where you stumble, there lies your treasure. The very cave you are afraid to enter turns out to be the source of what you are looking for. The damned thing in the cave, that was so dreaded, has become the centre.'

My first hideaway cave-time brought some relief, but I chose to enter a more challenging cave later. I went away for a few quiet days on my own to a retreat, ready to engage with the core of the pain and what might emerge from it.

Perhaps my initial crawl into a 'Cave of Defeat' was a necessary prelude to my willing step into the 'Cave of Retreat' — a second chamber where the surroundings could hold me gently in a safe, separate space and support my encounter with what felt like 'the damned thing'. Where we are willing, the cave in which we hide can become a place where we heal — a quiet place to process our pain in a protected environment; a place to go to pieces and slowly re- assemble our jigsawed selves.

I look back on my resisting self with more compassion now than I could receive or even offer myself back then. I hope I offer a little more patient acceptance for those caught up in the irrational behaviours and negative emotions of their own turbulent times.

No-one welcomes the pain of loss. But the only way through is to engage with the heart of the matter in the creative cave. We progress with kindness, going as slowly as we need to go, and without condemnation for how we are feeling.

Resistance is a defence that is trying to look after us, pushing back on the invasion of pain, in anger or distress at the tortuous gap between what we have and what we long for. Resistance does not want us to fall down that abyss, so it puts up a fight.

All this takes energy. Putting all our effort into resisting is, at best, wearying, and at worst, a door to other problems. Increasing attempts to numb ourselves, distract and insulate ourselves may temporarily subdue the pain but lead us into behaviours that are even more damaging — compulsive, driven, addictive. We need to re-direct our energies into reckoning with what is going on, rather than opposing it.

It can be hard to stop investing ourselves in patterns of resisting behaviour; those repeated attempts to achieve the same failing objective — to please an authority figure, attract a partner, regain full health, change a sibling. But if we are not to stay stuck, exhausted and frustrated, it is the only way to break the fruitless circle.

I found there came a point where whatever scenario I had to face could not be worse or more draining than constantly trying to push it away. I became determined to deal with my situation as it was — not as I wanted it to be or hoped I could make it.

Intentional letting go can bring a sense of mourning as we put to rest our desired goal, but it may also bring an unexpected feeling of relief. As we stop trying so hard, we become free to explore different options and our horizons widen. As someone once told me, 'I felt so much better when I gave up hope.'

This can be a time to access some therapeutic help, as we move into unknown territory. But the writing process may also be a support. The page is another separate space where we can express ourselves freely, engage honestly and explore creatively. As we read and reflect on the words we write, we become our own counsellor. Writing can help us shape and navigate our life, but sometimes it can be hard to know where to start.

What to Write

After my father died, my mother found a diary he had kept as a schoolboy. It was a printed pocket diary for 1942, with a small space allocated for each day. 'It wasn't a very eventful year', my mother memorably commented as she put it my hands. Life for a boarding school boy in the Lake District, it seemed, had a routine normality, Second World War notwithstanding.

In his working years, my father had a friend who kept a very fulsome, factual diary. He wrote it each morning on the commuter train to London. It was a triumph of record-keeping. If you wanted to know the local weather for any particular day in years past, he was the man to ask.

Whether we write briefly or at length, journalling is not the same as diary-writing. Unlike my father's dutiful filling of each dated diary space, a journal does not have to be written daily. Neither are there rules about what we 'ought' to include. Current weather conditions may be the thing for the meteorologically-inclined, but a journal is essentially a place to write about whatever is important to us.

My counselling clients sometimes expressed a desire to use writing to help them step back, take stock and incorporate a more reflective element into their lives. Some showed me their immaculate new journal bought for that purpose. But it was not unusual for them then to say, 'I've a lot of things going round in my head. I want to write. I just don't know what to write.'

Difficult times may pull us to the page. In the last chapter we noted James Pennebaker's research into writing about trauma. We may write to explore what distresses or disturbs us. But this is not our only journalling option.

Writing researcher Megan Hayes promotes the practice of positive journalling for wellbeing. Choosing to write about good experiences, to celebrate what is going well, and to develop an intentionally positive approach to our issues, can also move us along a healing pathway.

Human beings are naturally attuned to potential dangers around them, making our minds, in the words of psychologist Rick Hanson, 'Velcro for negative; teflon for positive'. Recording the positives gives them more substance and fosters a shift in perspective to a more balanced outlook. The Gratitude Journal — promoting the discipline of regularly writing down the specifics of what we are grateful for — has become a popular form of positive journalling. It strengthens our connection to what is good in our lives in the midst of all that is going on.

If we want to write about a big issue in our lives, we may be overwhelmed about where to start, but we do not have to tackle every aspect at once. There is nothing too big to address on the page, if we pace ourselves and write about it, step-by-step. We can slowly build the bigger picture by writing in manageable chunks, however small. Where everything feels chaotic or complex, we simply start exactly where we are, with what is currently on our plate. The writing process itself can bring greater clarity once we start moving the tangles in our head out onto the page, where we start to see their separate threads. But if there is nothing too big to write about, neither is there anything too small: that offhand remark or quote; that marginal incident; that tiny step we took towards our dreams; that fleeting moment that briefly took our breath away...

When apparently insignificant things make an impact that punches above their weight, they are likely to have touched something deeper, stirring somewhere in our unconscious. Writing may reveal that connection as something that surprises us — yet that we recognise — as it appears on our page. Small keys can open big doors.

If we want to write but do not know where to start, we can activate our pens by using our senses to take in what is around us and to note it down.

Recording what we see, hear, taste, touch and smell draws us gently into full attentiveness to the present moment.

As receptivity slows us down, we may find it easier to tune into our own being and inner world and give them a voice on the page: how does your body feel? What is occupying the space in your mind? Are you aware of a feeling around something that is hard to define, its origin elusive — an unsettledness, a dis-ease, happiness or sadness?

Writing around and about what is difficult to pinpoint can lead to some 'lightbulb moments', as we begin to formulate words for what is at the edge of our reach. Starting with the simplest of prompts, such as 'What is really going on?' can take us to fruitful places. Time and again, journallers have told me that as they begin to write about what is happening in their lives, they find unexpected new insight about what is going on underneath.

Choosing and using a prompt that appeals may be a helpful way to stimulate our writing. Online journalling prompts are plentiful, but the ones we devise for ourselves can be equally — and sometimes more — effective. A prompt may be a statement to reflect on or a question to explore. You may find that the statement-prompt and the question-prompt elicit different ways of writing.

We can build our own collection of prompts: a quote that sparks something in us; a question that interests us; an incident or memory that keeps coming to mind; a theme we want to explore. We may even find that our own previous journal entries yield some prompts for further exploration.

So what do you want to write? Take a few minutes to write about this. You may wish to write freely, or make a list of subjects. And as you may have already found, turning things around and writing about what you do not want to write about, may also be illuminating.

Marcela's Story: Writing to Express Emotions

Marcela's family circumstances gave her no shortage of material. She found writing to be a powerful resource in helping her maintain equilibrium through a difficult time.

Marcela was born and brought up in Chile. Although the family was affluent, life was not straightforward for Marcela and her sister. Their parents were often not there for them; Marcela's father's time was taken up not only with his business interests, but with his other women, to her mother's great distress and sometimes suicidal despair. Marcela found herself called upon to collude with her father's lies and to comfort her mother.

Bereft of parental nurture as she journeyed though adolescence, Marcela turned to writing to support herself. She filled diary after diary through her teenage years, writing about her feelings, exploring many uncertainties about her life, and her longings for escape. She found the writing process cathartic.

'It was a way to get things off my chest,' she says. 'I had a lively social life and loads of friends, but somehow it was writing things down rather than telling them that helped me through. A diary is like a good friend. No-one is there to judge what you say and what you feel.

'I wrote nearly every day, either at home, or by myself at the top of a hill behind our house in Santiago. I poured out my feelings — my anger towards my father and how I felt my mother did not need to suffer as she did.'

Though this happened a long time ago, Marcela has kept all her diaries. 'They are a precious source of memories from my past and upbringing. They are full of SO many feelings, even ones I had forgotten about, such as the love I had for my mother despite the dislike I have of the "victim" state. Reading what I have written rekindles some of those old emotions. I realise how much I was affected by what was going on in the family at the time.'

Marcela wrote an unsent letter to her father when she was fourteen. This is part of it, translated from its original Spanish:

'Is it such a great love that you have for us that my nerves are shattered because of your way of living that affects us all in the house and even the walls? More than once, I've thought about getting into strong drugs, to be a coward like both of you and escape from everyone and everything. But me, on my own, I am more aware than both of you together, because you escape with your women and Mum with her craziness. And I'm in the middle. But I'm not stupid. But if you want to throw shit at each other and I don't like what I see, why do I have to be in the middle? But I can't get out of the middle while I have to be here with you. But I feel very sad because neither of you give anything firm to stand on. You more than Mum. You scare me.

'There are moments when I feel sorry for you. I've stayed here because I pity you. How can it be for me that I have more pity than love for my parents? You've not known how to make decisions, and I'm up to here with it all…'

In the Resisting process, writing may help you to:

- Work around stuck emotions/reactions
- Discharge negative feelings safely
- Approach the intolerable in paced, safe way
- Name what you are experiencing
- Look at what you are defending
- Identify what is really going on
- Wrestle with a sense of powerlessness
- Clear the ground to go deeper

Journalling Suggestions

> Work around stuck emotions/reactions

Free-Writing What I Know

I am indebted to Nancy Kline's excellent book, *Time to Think*, for this suggestion. She suggests free-writing from the prompt: what do I know now that I am going to find out in a year's time?

This may sound a rather odd prompt, but the idea of it is to winkle out those things which we already are aware of in the most honest and deepest parts of us, but that we would really rather not look at and engage with now.

Personal writing has a wonderful capacity to help us shift perspective. If we write with that sense of 'in a year's time' on the horizon, it may distance our uncomfortable realisations sufficiently for us to be able to put them on the page in front of us. Through this slightly slanted approach, we may 'discover' more in our awareness than we would admit to head-on. This exercise can be done at any time, and is generally revealing and insightful.

As you re-read what you have written, you could use as a follow-up prompt: and what response does knowing this now invite me to make in the present moment?

This brings things closer back in, to challenge ourselves with present reality; it opens up an opportunity to take some small step or action that might start to address any underlying pressure or anxiety.

> Discharge negative feelings safely

A Dramatic Dialogue

A dialogue is one way of starting to work with something you identify as 'other.' You can write a dialogue with anyone or anything with which, or whom, you have some sort of issue or conflict. You can even set up a dialogue between different parts of yourself, capturing on paper the inner conversation one aspect of yourself is already having with another. When my knees were feeling particularly sore — as was I — after my osteoarthritis diagnosis, I wrote a dialogue with them.

A written dialogue can become a dynamic interchange, releasing insights that may not emerge from a more analytic approach. The idea is for each side to find out about the other, to speak freely and to listen attentively.

Set out your dialogue like a play script and start with some form of greeting. Continue by writing the conversation between your participants. When you are unsure what each one is going to say, just sit quietly and be open to their words emerging in their own time.

The central part of the dialogue focusses on each side speaking, and listening to where the other is coming from and what they really want to say. Each can ask the other about what they need or what would help them. Each needs to answer questions honestly, even if that answer is 'I don't know.' The idea is for both parties to come to some sort of truce, so they can accept one another and find a way of working together.

Finally, it can help if the two speakers sum things up in some parting words to one another.

Dialogue with Resistance

If it feels too much to tackle an issue directly, you could set up a dialogue with Resistance itself. Find out what is making Resistance tick, why it insists on showing up and doing what it does. How will you talk to Resistance — as a friend or an enemy?

Imagine you are sitting on a park bench, with two other figures sitting on your right. Immediately next to you is the rather bulky figure of Resistance. On the other side of them, and slightly obscured from your sight, is the thing you fear and are resisting.

What does Resistance look like to you? What are they wearing? Are they male, female or even a creature of some kind? Are they the strong, silent type? A bit of a thug or a smooth-talker?

Start a dialogue with Resistance. You know you need to talk to the figure blocked from view, but first, you know you need a conversation with Resistance, to negotiate changing places. It may take more than one conversation; you will have to gain Resistance's trust and agreement. What objections is Resistance putting up?

Use this dialogue with Resistance to find out more. Afterwards, you may be able to move on to talk with whatever Resistance is blocking — or with Resistance again, if they are reluctant to give way.

> Approach the intolerable in a safe way

Through the Cave

Earlier in this chapter, I wrote about the sort of cave we withdraw to as we hide from our situation of threat, and the sort of cave we retreat to in order to face our situation and find ways through it. Images can be powerfully evocative in enabling us to access and process deeper emotional material. This writing exercise is an imaginative fantasy that involves writing about two caves.

Imagine you are entering a cave that is the hiding place you know you can escape to at times of distress. Describe this hiding cave. What is it like? What do you find there to occupy you and help you shut out the world? Entertainment? Comfort? Describe what you see. Write about what it feels like to be here, drawing on all your senses.

In the corner, you notice an entrance that you know leads into the next chamber — a healing cave — but one where you know you will encounter that which you would rather avoid. What does this entrance look like? How do you feel as you see it? You are aware that this chamber contains a 'treasure' but also 'the dreaded thing'. How do you feel about entering it?

Something prompts you to go through into the healing cave; what is that — something stirring within you or something external that your senses pick up — a light, sound or smell?

As you enter, what do you see, hear, touch, smell and taste? Are you aware of encountering a 'dreaded thing' or the presence of treasure? Write about what happens next and what you do. Where does this writing take you? If you are not ready to go there, remember, you can pause your writing and re-enter the cave at any time.

> Name what you are experiencing

What I really…

Moving through the resisting process challenges us to get real about the situation we are in, instead of suppressing it or pushing it away. The set of sentence stems below is designed to prompt some more honest writing about what is really going on for us. You can complete each sentence one by one, and then write a few sentences of reflection on what you notice. Sometimes a series of sentences reveals an underlying thread or theme. If you identify one, this theme could then become a heading for a piece of free-writing.

You could also repeat the same sentence stem and finish it off in as many different ways as you can. Write continuously and freely, but set a limit of either time or on the number of sentences you will write. Do not worry if you repeat yourself; this is simply an indication of how important something is to you. Reflect on what has emerged and write a sentence or two to sum up your thoughts.

You will see that the last few sentence stems have a positive slant. Whether

Chapter 2: Resisting

you tackle all or some of these suggestions, finishing with more uplifting writing may help restore equilibrium if the earlier ones have generated more challenging material.

You could also invent some more 'really' sentence stems for yourself that would energise your own writing.

What I really want to say is
What I really feel is
What I really become bothered about is
What I really think is unfair is
What I really find it hard to talk about is
What I really don't want to happen is
What I really need is
What I really long for is
What I really like is
What I really find restorative is

Poetry Exploration

> Look at what you are defending

Resistance

The way that pebble lies
next to the seedling
pushing it one millimetre to the left
will (one day) shape the branches of the tree.

That pressure of sea wind
lets one leaf flourish *here*, withers another *there*,
until the whole thorn tree bows away from the ocean.
    And
this white page is not empty, but rather
occupied by all the small reluctances,
movements of spirit that bend me

to write *this* rather than *that.*
Sometimes when the wind blows
so bracingly my pen hesitates at
the clifftop of the page, and I close
the book and do not write.
   But
sometimes this resistance
is my guide, takes me to beauty
and to truth, the destination
of this daily pilgrimage, pushing
my face into the wind and rain.

Andrew Rudd

Any movement of growth or change encounters some form of resistance — from obstructing pebble to the pressure of a sea-wind. As with the poem's Speaker, our response can range from a small reluctance to a turning away in a refusal to act at all.

Where have you found yourself resisting, either on the page or in everyday life? Free-write about such a time for ten minutes, or to fill a page. What winds have proved just too bracing to face? Aim to explore, gently, what this might be about, without berating yourself.

Re-read what you have written and add a few sentences reflecting on any insights that have emerged. Could this writing help bring a strong resistance down to the level of a small reluctance? This will be enough to enable us to press on into 'the wind and rain'. In so doing, as the Speaker observes, we can find new avenues and alternative routes to what we seek. Resistance itself is transformed into a guide, not a barrier.

Have you known a time when you have persevered, reluctance notwithstanding, and found a fresh, creative — and perhaps surprising — way forward? Write about this experience of, as it were, resisting the *resistance.*

Trust that it can happen again as you turn to a current issue buffeted by a cliff-top wind or pressured by small reluctances. Set an intention to 'face into the wind and rain' and keep writing — or taking steps forward — to discover fresh ways around or through. And allow the destination to take time to appear; a seedling does not become a tree overnight.

Chapter 2: Resisting

> Identify what is really going on

Sparrow Legs

Just before sunrise birds stir,
herald the dawn once more
to the rhythm of the solitary runner
whose trainers beat on asphalt.
Drum-taut calves pulse on automaton legs
that syncopate in sudden spins
into side-streets where
birds' unblinking eyes watch him
Stop.

He leans over, hands gripping thighs
as lungs clutch at air.
No spare breath for song.
His mind races its well-worn track,
press-gangs the body
for its next onslaught at outrunning
the burning words, the nickname
his old PE teacher kindled so casually:
Sparrow Legs.

A moment's wit; a branding down decades.
Seventeen marathons on,
Shame's after-glow still flares his face
as he strains over finishing lines that bring
No Ending.

This poem was inspired by a piece in a TV programme about a man who had poured years of time and energy into long-distance running in an effort to disprove what his school PE teacher had once called him. This was not running for pleasure. Completing a marathon did not settle the score nor bring him relief. His life had 'no spare breath for song'.

In a resisting process, we respond to a perceived threat by trying to push it away. This may work in the short term, but it leaves the situation stuck. As they say, keep trying the same thing over and over again and you will get the same results.

Like the birds, become an observer of this runner and write your reflections on the following questions:

What do you think his running is really about?

What does he not wish to face? Fear — merited or groundless? Powerlessness? Pain?

What other factors in this situation, present and past, might he see if he stopped long enough to look?

What else might he do rather run himself into the ground?

It is often easier to deal with resistance in another than in ourselves, so turn the bird's eye towards yourself. Are there things you know you do to avoid facing the intolerable? It can be intense and compulsive consumption of food, drink, shopping, entertainment, or pressing on with the same old fruitless battle.

Write a letter to yourself as your own best and kindest friend, naming your vulnerabilities with compassion, and suggesting some gentle, constructive ways forward to break any wearying patterns of resistance.

The runner from the poem was featured in a programme about forgiveness. In it, he wrote to his old PE teacher about what had happened, his feelings and his willingness to forgive him. The teacher received the letter kindly, but was bemused, as he had no memory of the event. How does knowing that make you feel?

> Wrestle with a sense of powerlessness

Blessing in the Chaos

To all that is chaotic
in you,
let there come silence.

Let there be
a calming
of the clamoring,
a stilling
of the voices that
have laid their claim

on you,
that have made their
home in you,

that go with you
even to the
holy places
but will not
let you rest,
will not let you
hear your life
with wholeness
or feel the grace
that fashioned you.

Let what distracts you
cease.
Let what divides you
cease.
Let there come an end
to what diminishes
and demeans,
and let depart
all that keeps you
in its cage.

Let there be
an opening
into the quiet
that lies beneath
the chaos,
where you find
the peace
you did not think
possible
and see what shimmers
within the storm.

Jan Richardson

This poem is a blessing for those in upheaval. When we resist what we do not want to accept, our inner world can become quite noisy and disordered. Our struggles with inner disruption may also spill over into our relationships with others.

The key repetition in this poem is the word 'let'. The emphasis is on allowing a different response in yourself, rather than doing or actively trying to make something happen.

Are there areas of your life where you sense a need to rest or let go? Mirroring the poem above, write a series of short lines where each sentence begins with the word 'Let' and see where that takes you. What do you imagine are the consequences of letting go? What might shimmer in the storm?

Amidst the chaos, the poet writes of *silence, wholeness and peace.* Choose one of these and write about what this means to you at the moment. You can write either as prose or in the form of poetry — perhaps using the short, fragmentary style used above.

How does setting your words out in this way, with so much white space around them, affect the impact of what you are writing as you read it back for yourself?

> Clear the ground to go deeper

Ask Me

Some time when the river is ice ask me
mistakes I have made. Ask me whether
what I have done is my life. Others
have come in their slow way into
my thought, and some have tried to help
or to hurt: ask me what difference
their strongest love or hate has made.

I will listen to what you say.
You and I can turn and look
at the silent river and wait. We know
the current is there, hidden; and there

are comings and goings from miles away
that hold the stillness exactly before us.
What the river says, that is what I say.

William Stafford

Although we have looked at the dynamic emotions of 'Resistance', sometimes this quality emerges as ice rather than fire — an intentional rigidity that arms us against the vulnerable places underneath, as armour coats flesh. In this poem, the Speaker observes the frozen river as an image of their own life.

Begin a free-write from the line 'Some time when the river is ice'. Think about how the river has responded to the drop in temperature in the environment. What is the temperature change in your world that results in a freezing over?

What emotion does the poem evoke in you as you read it aloud?

Where in your body/heart/mind/soul might you need a little thawing, some free-flow?

In what ways have or do you numb yourself to your situation?

As you think about where you feel frozen and immobile, imagine you can sense the 'comings and goings from miles away', which are working beneath the surface. What shifts for you when you bring into your awareness the presence of hidden currents?

What does the river say as you wait and listen?

When you find yourself…	Writing may help you to…
• Persisting with old strategies	• Work around stuck emotions/ reactions
• Angry at self/others/situation	• Discharge negative feelings safely
• Pushing voices away that echo the truth	• Approach the intolerable in a safe way
• Fighting emotional battles	• Name what you are experiencing
• Feeling defensive	• Look at what you are defending
• Refusing to consider other outcomes	• Identify what is really going on
• Feeling unjustly done by	• Wrestle with a sense of powerlessness
• Looking for magical solutions	• Clear the ground to go deeper

Chapter 3: Reckoning

- Needing comfort or support
- Disillusioned and sad
- Accepting loss in current situation
- Feeling ungrounded
- Aware of complex emotions
- Sitting with this season
- Sensing you are in an alien landscape
- Acknowledging fears and uncertainty

When Janet's husband Paul[1] died suddenly of a heart attack in his early 40s, she was left to bring up their two young teenage sons on her own. Coming to terms with her loss was as challenging as it was hard to take in. For a long time afterwards, she said it seemed as though Paul was just away on a business trip.

'I felt that at any moment I might hear the sound of his car on the drive, and see him walking in at the back door,' she said. 'Then somehow, one day, it finally sank in. He was never coming home.'

Joseph Campbell, the mythologist who studied the trajectory of the archetypal hero's journey observes: 'We must be willing to let go of the life we've planned, so as to have the life that is waiting for us.' In the hero's journey, the hero chooses to take on a quest and venture out in pursuit of a dream, leaving the old familiar life behind. In the unwanted journey, our old life and dreams leave us. Our first task is simply to assent to the reality of this new territory, into which we have been thrust.

Janet had moved beyond reacting to, and resisting, her situation; she was willing to come to terms with the fact of Paul's death. As this conscious acceptance percolated through her subconscious, it enabled a momentous shift into the reckoning process.

---

[1] Names changed

Whether this acceptance starts as a conscious decision, or whether it is more of an emerging acquiescence to the reality of life in the present moment, such a mindset can work in us at a deep level. Janet was able to assent to its natural unfolding within her as her loss took its course. She recognised that an inner change had taken place, without her trying to force it.

We can balk at accepting our situation because we fear this means approving the very thing that appals us. Acceptance can feel like settling for defeat, rather than fighting on to that elusive victory we are determined to achieve. But the letting go that is acceptance is not a resigned waving of the white flag. In this scenario, surrender is victory. Acceptance is an act of courage. We stop fighting fruitless battles to regroup and redirect our energies. The spiritual teacher and writer Eckhart Tolle notes that sometimes: 'Letting things go is an act of far greater power than defending or hanging on.'

There is a time to press on and wrestle through obstacles, and a time to pull back and walk away. Knowing which response fits the situation takes some discernment, but if hanging on to something means going round in circles and becoming drained to no avail, it may be time to dare to let go.

Acceptance of something challenging is not often achieved instantly; it is a process that can take time. We may find we need to persevere in our choice to let go, only later realising that we are truly set on a new course.

Over the years, Gordon and I have made several climbs up Red Pike, the majestic peak which stands at one end of Lake Buttermere. As my knee osteoarthritis worsened, I reflected on how I could not see a time when I would ever climb it again. Then one day, I suddenly caught myself thinking, 'but there are other Red Pikes!'

Everything I put into scrambling and pressing uphill to enjoy the clear air and panoramic views could be reconfigured. From the physical hills I had walked, I could take the energy and desire to climb — the willingness to explore; the persistence to keep going after a stumble; the skills of picking a pathway along rocky trails — and transpose them all to a different aspect of living, abandoning the current false trail.

The paradox of acceptance is that by calling a truce with the realities of our situation, we can open the door to engaging with them in a new way. Acceptance unlocks creative possibilities closed to us while we were fixated on one particular outcome. Now, we are free to find other ways forward, even if it is hard to muster up the enthusiasm for them just yet.

As my mother and mother-in-law aged and started to struggle with walking, I was saddened at how both shunned the aids that could help them. For every mobility scooter out and about, I guess there are more than a few gathering dust. Whether pride or fear is behind that refusal to accept and adapt to changed circumstances, it consigns one to going nowhere, rather than being able to go somewhere *now*, even if not everywhere as before. I hope I am able to engage more positively as, if, and when, my own challenges come. Acceptance may feel like an ending that calls time on hope, but it is a turning point that resonates with the wartime words of Winston Churchill: 'This is not the end. It is not even the beginning of the end. But it may be the end of the beginning.'

In a reckoning process, what exactly might be beginning is hidden; our more immediate sense may be one of disillusionment, alongside a new uncertainty about our identity. If our identity has become very wedded to what we most desire to gain or keep — job, status, achievement, person, situation — then the issue of who we are and whom we shall become when we let it go can leave us feeling very vulnerable. We can feel at a loss, wondering who and where we are now.

We may have become attached even to the prospect of a dream fulfilled, used to living on-hold, thinking that everything will be all right when we: have this child, lose this weight, find a partner, leave a partner, get a clear bill of health; some longed-for recognition, and so on. Yet, acceptance means being in the present with these unresolved things.

Letting go of our focus on a goal once so clear can bring up a sense of anxiety at our lack of direction; however, we do not have to get or be anywhere else but here and now, accommodating our emotions as we catch up with the wholeness of ourselves in this place. Unsettledness is part of the territory. In the wise words of the poet T S Eliot:

In order to arrive at what you are not
You must go through the way in which you are not?

With unwanted journeys, the way forward unfolds step by step, with no clear map or time table. It is less a matter of pinpointing a destination, more of navigating our way through what is around us. We set a direction, and listen and look around and within us to discern where to place the next step. For many of us, this is a new way of travelling.

Such a journey has its own momentum. There is a rhythm of stepping forward and resting up; no inertia, but also no urgency. As acceptance befriends our situation, our current circumstances no longer have the last word.

In his book *Obliquity*, the academic economist John Kay asserts that the best destinations are reached via an indirect approach. We rarely know enough to ensure the success of any enterprise, however meticulously planned; we need to be prepared to make adjustments en route, as unforeseen factors emerge and earlier assumptions prove hollow. The most important thing to attend to is making the wisest next step, trusting that the path will emerge as we risk moving forward, making discoveries and learning on the way. Kay advises that when faced with 'a task that daunts you, a project you find difficult, begin by doing something…a small component that seems potentially relevant'.

In the reckoning process, we may feel that this is all we are actually able to do. It is a way of *being* described by the poet Naomi Shihab Nye in *White Silk* as:

'The lifelong vocation of standing wherever you are and knowing which way to walk next.'

These early steps of acceptance can feel reluctant and tentative.

A few months after our final infertility treatment was scheduled, Gordon and I were due to take up our annual invitation to speak and lead worship on a Christian travel company's skiing holiday. I viewed our earlier agreement as purely provisional; my assumption was that I would have to withdraw from that commitment well before the event.

When treatment floundered, we confirmed we could both go. It was a bitter-sweet 'yes', accompanied by some tears. I felt I was dragging my feet along this path in lead boots, but it was the one open to me; I could choose to say 'yes' to this lovely opportunity as the gift of the moment, amidst the disappointment of it not being what I had asked for. It felt like a step away from what I wanted and I had no clear idea of what it was a step towards — if anything. It was just the next constructive thing to do.

Chapter 3: Reckoning

In the reckoning process, we enter liminal space — the word 'liminal' deriving from the Latin word 'limen' or 'threshold', the territory of in-between. Now we are resolving to peel away from the old life and face into the uncertainty of what may lie ahead. This space holds much potential for something new to emerge, but we encounter it first as an 'edge-land' — a nameless place out on the margins of town.

Finding our own words for our experience can help us start to ground ourselves even here, giving substance to the shapes in the mist. Even if we do not know where we are going, we can begin to reckon with where we are. It is a good time to put pen to paper.

When to write

When is the best time to plant a tree? The answer, of course, is 'twenty years ago'. So, when is the next best time? Now! When we discover how helpful personal writing can be, we may wish we had started earlier, but the open page of today lies before you. You need not wait until you area 'good enough' writer, with a journalling qualification and an ability for flawless spelling. Having some sense of why you want to write and perhaps a prompt or two to suggest what you might write about is enough. You are ready to make a start. There is no special, 'magical' hour to get going. One of the beauties of writing is its accessibility; you can pick up a pen at any time of day or night. The page can also be a companion whenever you need to offload a feeling or explore an issue but have no-one else to talk to.

As my journalling group discussed when they wanted to write, one responded with a single word: 'regularly'. We have already noted that a journal need not be written daily in order to be of value, but it does help to be writing frequently enough to maintain momentum.

Continuity of practice offers more long-term benefit than the occasional drop-in. You may decide to take a spontaneous approach, journalling when something has arisen that prompts your desire to write. You may be a planner who prefers to set aside specific writing times.

Personally, I have found it most fruitful to establish an underlying journalling rhythm, with regular, planned anchor-points (such as a weekly review). This allows some flexibility to be a little more fluid with my entries in-between. The advantage of a set writing routine is that it primes your subconscious; material you have been carrying around inside is more likely to emerge when it senses you are ready to welcome it, as you honour your writing appointment, come what may.

When you write is an individual decision in the light of what works best for you. It does not matter whether you are a morning lark or a night owl journaller, but it is worth bearing in mind that writing at different times of day — or night — can have a bearing on the nature of that writing.

Morning writing tends to be more forward-looking, with content focussed around planning and intention-setting. Writing should happen very early in the morning if you want to capture the content of a vivid dream or some overnight inspiration as soon as you wake.

Writing in the evening offers a better opportunity to review your day, and may be more reflective. Some find it helpful to write last thing at night, perhaps even in bed. This can be a time to note the day's positives; to write down worries so their weight rests on the page rather than the mind; to set a reminder of what to pick up on when waking — and what to leave behind.

Though morning and/or evening journalling can form satisfying frames to the day, your particular circumstances may suggest a different time as being better for you. Perhaps there is a point in the day when you know the house is quiet or another space, or place, in your routine that could be an opportunity for some uninterrupted writing.

You do not have to set aside a long block of time. A few minutes for a couple of lines may be all that is needed for those short entries, brief jottings, a memorable quote, important thought or something you have noticed. Small can be beautiful — and powerful. Giving yourself permission to start short can help you sustain your journalling more effectively than feeling daunted at having to write at length — and then never writing at all. You may find that some of those brief journal entries expand as you move naturally into taking more time to write.

It is also worth being aware of your state of mind as you write. Distress or sorrow, agitation or anger may have prompted you to pick up your pen; they may even emerge as you are engaged in the writing itself. Writing can re-connect you to some strong feelings. It is helpful to put emotions into words and discharge them in the safe place of the page to support yourself through difficult experiences. It is natural that in so doing, you may experience some discomfort. However, if emotions become too disturbing and threaten to overwhelm, it does not help to press on relentlessly. We need to know when to stop. There is a time not to write, as well as a time to write. We do not want to entrench ourselves in an emotional rut. Nor do we have to completely process a complex issue in one sitting. The page is patient and does not judge our pace of progress. It simply waits for us to return to write when we are ready.

Part of James Pennebaker's rationale of a 15-20 minute limit on free-writing is to set a time boundary that protects trauma-writers from becoming overwhelmed. You may wish to set your own writing boundaries. This could be around time or even space, for example, allowing yourself to write to the bottom of just one or two pages.

Timing, as well as time, is important. If your journey's onset has been marked by trauma, you need to take particular care. Pennebaker advises that it is best to wait a month or two before writing directly about trauma; there need be no rush to process events. Creating a little distance from the original shock will shift perspective enough to enable you to write about it, and through it, more fruitfully. Go gently and pace yourself kindly.

So, take some time to write about when you will write, and about what would make it a time not to write. You may want to experiment with writing at different times to see how that impacts your writing. Which are the easiest and which the most challenging times? How can you best put in place, and commit to, the times most natural to you?

You could explore what emerges when you approach your writing time in a way less conducive to you. If you are a planner, take a week when you allow yourself to journal more spontaneously, in response to feeling, intention, incident or inspiration — rather than the clock. If you prefer to go with the flow, try a week of committing to set times. Finally, you may want to make your own checklist of times not to write, whether because the environment or timing is not helpful, or when what you need to do is not to write but to look after yourself in some other way.

Francesca's Story: Developing a Writing Practice

Francesca has been living with anorexia since she was a teenager. These days, she works with words professionally in various capacities, as a journalist and storyteller. She writes about eating disorders for publication, noting that whilst part of her worries about what others may think, she wants to be honest and transparent about her own situation.

As a young adult, Francesca spent over a year in a psychiatric hospital. For the first couple of months, she was very resistant, and says, 'It felt as though I was in enforced lockdown.' Eventually, she realised she needed to accept where she was, and just 'get on with it'. Writing became an essential personal support. Francesca started to keep a daily journal, which gradually 'became a friend'. Her journal was somewhere to turn to when she needed someone to talk to. She could use it to disclose her feelings and to clarify her thinking.

Francesca's journalling mostly takes the form of free-writing, perhaps up to two or three pages at a time. She enjoys being active and out and about, and confesses to finding outer activity a way of distracting herself. So, writing is a useful discipline to turn herself back in on her thoughts, as she journals both positive and negative experiences.

Whilst living in hospital, Francesca explored writing aspects of her story as a novel and memoir. Her journal entries formed a basis for this creative angle, and she keeps them as a source for further personal writing. She says she is reluctant to re-read what she has written for its own sake, feeling that getting too close to the vividness of earlier trauma could trigger some distress; she can best stay resilient by remaining slightly detached from her personal writing.

Francesca journals about matters past and future, as well as present. 'I have an annual review of what I want to accomplish in my life, in different areas. Writing helps make things concrete. The writing process is so accessible. All it needs is a pen and paper, and most of us can do it. Writing is so obvious and ordinary that we tend to forget how helpful it can be.'

Excerpt From Francesca's narrative, *Waking Up*

The hospital grounds are quiet and desolate. Brick buildings fashioned through the early half of the last century stand beside prefabricated and shoddy structures, their decay echoed in the scent of the large green overflowing bins. This is the kind of place where people could easily be forgotten about. It is still, isolated, not like any hospital I have been to

Chapter 3: Reckoning

before. I think of the frantic rush of an ordinary hospital, where Accident & Emergency teems with people and a sense of urgency. Here there is no speed, no urgency, no one seems compelled to do anything. On the way in I noted a vending machine, lop-sided and ageing, empty bar one bottle of water with a fading label. 'Even the vending machine is anorexic.' I laughed to myself.

As I sit eating my sodden Weetabix, I wonder what belonging in a mental hospital looks like. Are there certain behaviours that are expected of me? Should I start crying over my cereal? Why is the nurse staring intently? I run my fingers through my hair.

I had brushed it quickly when waking, but now am not sure whether it looks a mess, or is too tidy. Are crazy people meant to bother with their appearance? Not that I'm bothering, looking down to my dishevelled pyjamas and screwed up bed linen upon which I sit.

The battered plastic tray and carefully measured portions, labelled with scrawled biro on shreds of yellow Post-it notes remind me of grandfather's nursing home. I am now no different to him. All adult responsibilities removed, and to be observed whilst eating, peeing, washing and not allowed to leave my room. They even confiscated my tweezers, presumably concerned I will pluck myself to oblivion.

When the final crumbs and drops of my breakfast have been consumed I look up. 'So what happens now?' I ask.

In the Reckoning process, writing may help you to:

- Contain difficult feelings
- Express your sorrow in a safe place
- Say goodbye to old dreams
- Re-connect to the substance of daily life
- Name and arrange conflicting feelings
- Validate your situation
- Gently re-connect with the world
- Find a framework for disorder

Journalling Suggestions

> Contain difficult feelings

Lists

Lists can be written about anything from immediate practicalities, such as a to-do or shopping list, to longer-term ambitions. They may reflect aspects of thinking and feeling, as well as doing.

A list is a useful way to collect material quickly, jotting down individual words or short phrases; afterwards, you can re-order them, set priorities, or pick out the elements that are calling for a little more attention. Writing a list of things you find difficult can enable you to take that first step in naming and acknowledging an issue. The list will contain it until you are ready to look at it more deeply.

A to-do list sets intentions for the upcoming day's action, but you can also write lists that look back over the day just passed. This might be a list of things you:

- Have achieved
- Are grateful for
- Are glad you have done
- Were surprised about (or delighted, or frustrated, or challenged, etc.)
- Made a choice about
- Want to do differently tomorrow

You could choose several of the above, or devise your own list for whatever you want to track. You may limit your list to, say, three, five or ten things; you may prefer to list freely for as long as it takes to complete what you want to put down.

After a few days, re-read and review your lists. What do you notice? Do any themes or repeating items emerge? What impact, if any, do you think writing these things down at the end of one day has had on the next? Write a few sentences to sum up your reflections.

As well as looking back or looking forward, lists can also register things in the present moment. Write a list of things you feel vulnerable about just now. Write as things occur to you, without judging them or trying to rank them in order. Afterwards, re-read this list. What do you notice? Do you see any patterns or groupings of items? Write a few sentences reflecting on your list and any insights or direction it suggests to you.

Simply listing vulnerabilities without elaborating on them can help shift perspective. The uncomfortable feelings may remain, but writing down what is triggering them corrales these things on the page. As you look at them, their sense of threat can be reduced, freeing you to find ways of managing the risks and the opportunities they may present.

> Express your sorrow in a safe place

The Unsent Letter

From thank-you notes to work e-mails, we all have some familiarity with written correspondence.

The unsent letter has a more open structure than a list. Its framework leaves plenty of space for creative imagination and expression, but it still has its conventions: the opening greeting and final sign-off, clear sentences and paragraphs, and a conversational tone. Though not as dramatically interactive as a dialogue, it also has no limit on whom or what it engages. You can write an unsent letter or e-mail to anyone or anything: a person — living or dead, a situation, an aspect of yourself, a body part, the past or future you. It might even be a letter of farewell to a way of living, a person, place, job or income.

You write to whomever or whatever you want to say something: words of gratitude, explanation or anger; words you wish you had said; or words you cannot say face-to-face. Expressing these things can help your internal processing of an issue. To be effective, your letter must be authentic and tell it like it is — which is why it is unsent. (Though it may form the basis for working on a letter that would be appropriate to send.) Think about what you will do with this letter afterwards. Reflect on it? Keep it? Shred it?

You could take this a step further and use your imagination to write the other side's reply. Afterwards, note down any insights that emerge from this angle.

> Say 'goodbye' to old dreams

Quotations as Prompts

What does letting go mean to you? Below are some quotations reflecting on the issue:

'Let reality be reality. Let things flow naturally forward in whatever way they like.'
Lao Tzu

'Let go of certainty. The opposite isn't uncertainty. It's openness, curiosity and a willingness to embrace paradox.'
Tony Schwartz

'To let go is to release the images and emotions, the grudges and fears, the clinging and disappointments of the past that bind our spirit.'
Jack Kornfield

'I am not what happened to me. I am what I choose to become.'
Carl Jung

'Let go of your attachment to being right, and suddenly your mind is more open.'
Ralph Marston

'Letting go means to come to the realisation that some people are part of your history, but not a part of your destiny.'
Steve Maraboli

And from an anonymous source:

'To let go is to admit powerlessness, which means that the outcome is not in my hands…'

'To let go is not to "care for", but to "care about".'

'To let go is not to adjust everything to my desires, but to take each day as it comes and cherish myself in it.'

Use these quotations as a stimulus for your own reflective writing — or you may wish to search for one of your own. Is there one that stands out for you? Perhaps you agree with it. Perhaps you would argue against it. Take the quotation and add it as the heading at the top of your page. Underneath, free-write for several minutes. Afterwards, re-read your writing. What do you notice? Where has it taken you? Is there a 'note to self' that you want to take away from the writing you have done?

Chapter 3: Reckoning

> Re-connect to the substance of daily life

The Heart of the Day

When we feel directionless and ungrounded, journalling can help us re-connect with what is of substance in our lives. Rather than trying to cover all bases, we narrow our focus onto what matters most. In this activity, we simply write about the heart of our day.

Look back over your day and reflect on what is your most stand-out moment. It may be an important event you had planned or something quite incidental. It is most likely to be linked to your day's strongest emotion. Perhaps you have felt frustrated by a problem you could not solve; uplifted at seeing something beautiful; anxious about something you needed to do; delighted at that unexpected phone call from an old friend. As you sit quietly, allow the heart of your day to surface.

Now free-write for a few minutes on what has come to mind. Describe this moment and the feeling it engendered. Continue to explore the story underneath this feeling. What has made this moment particularly significant for you? What is it about?

Afterwards, re-read your writing and see what you notice. Finally, write a note to self about how you want to respond. Is this moment something to let go of or to savour?

Perhaps it suggests an action you want to take tomorrow.

Poetry Exploration

> Name and arrange conflicting feelings

The Gift

Not long after, I lost it.
Loveliest of things,
        hand-stitched,
so soft and subtle I barely knew it was there.

Ask me now
and though I could tell you
                              just when and where I first saw
it,
how it became essential is hard
                              and how it slipped from me
harder still.

A last moment of neglect
or something slower,
                    more insidious,
the way, warp and weft,
a face, a voice, is sewn right in.
It was possession made me careless.

Maura Dooley

This poem grieves the loss of something precious, albeit something that had come to be taken for granted. We are not told exactly what the object was, but we do know that it was special — 'hand-stitched' and with personal connections woven into its very fabric. This 'loveliest of things' had become *essential* and its loss brings up a range of feelings: sorrow; affection for those personal connections; joy at the gift's beauty; regret, and perhaps self-blame, at having lost it. In the poem, these feelings are expressed, arranged and held.

As you reckon with the loss of something precious, you may experience a range of complicated or even conflicting feelings. Write about what you have lost, allowing these feelings to be included in your writing as they make themselves known. You may wish to write in phrases and fragments, arranging your words across the page's white space in the manner of the poem. Name the feelings that emerge, simply accepting them without censoring them or condemning or justifying yourself. It is enough for now to let them rest on the page as you bring them into the light.

The poem's last line gently prompts us to cherish what we have now. Reflect on your life at the moment. Loss notwithstanding, what gift or gifts are in danger of being taken for granted? Is possession making you careless? What do you want to pay more attention to as a gift to you now?

Write about the gift or gifts in your life and explore how you can cherish them. Setting this down on the page can remind you that these gifts are still preciously present, whatever other difficulties you face.

> Validate your situation

Everything Has Its Time

1 For everything there is a season and a time for every matter under heaven:

2 a time to be born and a time to die;
a time to plant and a time to pluck up what is planted;

3 a time to kill, and a time to heal;
a time to break down and a time to build up;

4 a time to weep, and a time to laugh;
a time to mourn and a time to dance;

5 a time to throw away stones and a time to gather stones together;
a time to embrace and a time to refrain from embracing;

6 a time to seek and a time to lose;
a time to keep and a time to throw away;

7 a time to tear and a time to sew;
a time to keep silence and a time to speak;

8 a time to love and a time to hate;
a time for war and a time for peace.

(From Ecclesiastes, Chapter 3)

The writer of this perhaps familiar passage from the Bible takes an eternal perspective on life's temporalities. We may have little control of the seasons through which our life-journey passes, but the acceptance of the season we are in can bring a consolation and/or a cherishing of its unique time.

Lectio Divina has been practised as a daily discipline by monastic communities down the centuries as a way of reading a sacred text. Its slow savouring and receptive attentiveness is transposable to the reading of poetry, inviting a deeper encounter of heart and spirit. Try taking a *Lectio Divina* approach to the poetry of Ecclesiastes above by reading the words through, slowly, several times. As you read, listen out for the word, phrase or line that particularly catches your attention. What is it your time to do?

Reflect on your response; especially its emotional pulse. Does your phrase prompt a sense of recognition, discovery, consolation or even irritation? What is it stirring within? When you have sat with this phrase for a while, write it out on the page.

What words do you want to write beneath it? Poetic lines that follow on? The start of a free-write? Perhaps you find yourself taking issue with the writer and want to write a letter to, or a dialogue with, them.

Afterwards, re-read what you have written, noting any insights that have emerged, aware of the assertion of St John of the Cross, that 'Words can do for the heart what light can do for a field.'

> Gently re-connect to the world

Wayfarer

Fledglings squawk — open their yellow
rimmed beaks in an under-eaves nest.

A feather floats down on cushioned air —
there is nothing rushed in its descent.

Luminous under dark trees it parachutes
onto a blood beetle who is oblivious.

Shifted by gusts of wind it kisses,
pauses on humus rich earth.

Held in the vane, a bead of rain kindles
sparks of a reflected tangerine sun.

Feather flutters over white-lipped
snails to the mist-sizzling river

to become a miniature coracle
that spins along behind a map of leaves.

Diana Sanders

In this poem, the Speaker describes a feather's drift from a fledgling's nest to the river's current below. Each stage of its descent is attentively observed in short, two-line stanzas amid the page's white space. As we read it, the poem slows our pace to match the feather's.

When we take time to focus on something in our environment and put words to what we notice, it slows us down as writers, too; we develop our capacity to pay attention as we release thoughts of things past or future to engage with the rich depths of the present moment.

Seek out something that is moving slowly. It might be an animal — a stalking cat, soaring bird, swimming fish or crawling insect. It could be an object carried by air or water. Or a human being — a young child or older person, a leisurely, or even lost, individual. Watch closely and notice how they move. Track their varying pace, what prompts them into motion, their relationship to their environment.

As with *Wayfarer*, shape your writing into a series of two-line stanzas, with each line between five and eight lines long. You will need to be selective and specific in your word choices.

Pay particular attention to how you describe movement. *Wayfarer*'s feather floats, parachutes and pauses, flutters and spins. How does your subject move?

Afterwards, write a sentence or two reflecting on how you have experienced this exercise.

> Find a framework for disorder

Growth

A glance inside the wardrobe shows it
Bursting at the seams with
Clothes, all crammed in together
Dark hangers jostle for position

Ever tighter like the rush hour tube
Fuller than the recommended weight load
Getting older isn't easy
Having to go up a dress size (or two)
Isn't
Joyous
Knowing the scales don't
Lie even if you find excuses
Many more
New items bought as
Of necessity you adjust but
Procrastinate about disposal
Quietly hoping that *one day* you will
Resolutely
Slip back into that smaller size
Treachery to think not
Until it dawns that *downsizing* is a
Vastly ambitious term
Wishful thinking like
Xray vision has its seeds in fantasy
You pack them away *out of sight out of mind* until
the Zeal wears off

Pauline Bell

Growth is written in the form of an Alphabet poem. An alphabet poem offers the creative opportunity of a framework; it only requires that you begin the first word of each line with the next letter of the alphabet. The lines themselves may be complete units, single words, or parts of longer phrases or sentences that run through several lines. *Growth* illustrates all of these possibilities. Within this form, the poem can be reflective as well as descriptive.

Write your own alphabet poem. The possibilities are endless. You could focus on an object or aspect of the natural world — from a waterfall to winter, from moorland to a mouse. You could write more directly about an issue or person, memory or aspiration, a place or time in your life. *Growth* tackles something the Speaker is thinking through, as it tracks the letters of the alphabet. The form brings a light touch to something that could be quite dispiriting.

Chapter 3: Reckoning

Writing an alphabet poem can be absorbing, challenging and energising. Completing the pattern can bring us pleasure; we may also find that its constraints open up a creativity, insight or angle we might not have found otherwise.

If you find the alphabet poem a fruitful exercise, you could also try your hand at its sister form — the Acrostic poem. The acrostic poem works on the same principle of dictating the starting letter of each line; only this time, each letter is part of the word or phrase you have chosen as your title. For example, you might choose 'Acceptance'.

Under your title, write ACCEPTANCE vertically in the left-hand margin of your page, with a new line for each letter, in sequence. Now all you need to do is to complete the rest of the lines and the poem…

When you find yourself…

- Needing comfort or support
- Disillusioned and sad
- Accepting of loss in current situation
- Feeling ungrounded
- Aware of complex emotions
- Sitting with *this* season
- Sensing you are in an alien landscape
- Acknowledging fears and uncertainty

Writing may help you to…

- Contain difficult feelings
- Express your sorrow in a safe place
- Say goodbye to old dreams
- Re-connect to the substance of daily life
- Name and arrange conflicting feelings
- Validate your situation
- Gently re-connect to the world
- Find a framework for disorder

Writing the Journeys We Never Wanted to Make

Chapter 4: Re-orientating

- Willing to adapt to new parameters
- Starting to explore changed world
- Looking for what one can, not cannot, do
- Asking many questions — with few answers
- Adrift amid unexpected possibilities
- Living with uncertainty of outcome
- Loosening loyalty to an outdated story
- Opening up to new knowledge

'I can feel your frustration, but I'm afraid the answer is "no".' The Consultant looked me directly in the eye. 'There is a time for the operation, but it's not yet.' I felt powerless. I had expressed my wish for the knee replacement surgery I hoped would bring permanent pain relief and a restored ease of mobility. A friend who had had this operation described in glowing terms how it 'gives you your life back'. But not for me, it seemed. Apparently, I would have to get worse before surgery became an option to make things better.

'You're bad, but not that bad,' said the Consultant. He handed me a self-help leaflet.

Oh yes, I knew that one, with its handy pull-out back-flap illustrating a helpful range of exercises: four on a bed, two with a chair, one on the stairs. Been there, done those and got the t-shirt. 'We'll make an appointment for you in six months,' said the Consultant. 'But come back before then if you need to.'

'What would be the point of that?' I thought. I had been asked what I wanted and then told I could not have it. I seethed as I came out of the consulting room, making a beeline for the hospital café and some comfort consumption.

At the first sip of my cappuccino, I sensed the small but firm inner voice of inconvenient truth: 'They're right, you know,' it said. I knew in my heart of hearts I was not ready emotionally or physically for the intervention of major surgery. And to be honest, I had not yet fully lost the life that others said they got back.

So what now? I could wait for my condition to worsen, putting my life on hold for some indeterminate time till the day when surgery would hopefully get it moving again. I could push against the Consultant's verdict and insist on this operation somewhere, somehow. Or, I could take a fresh look at where I had landed and see what new choices might lie within these seemingly unshifting parameters.

The cul-de-sacs of an unwanted journey can leave us feeling trapped. As limits close in and options run out, stress rises up. But this can be the moment to take a deep breath and engage, with re-orientation.

In the re-orientating process, we slow down and give ourselves time to take stock; to consider different perspectives and be open to thinking outside the box. We cannot re-orientate in a rush, if we want to discover what choices we do have; hidden possibilities are not always quick to reveal themselves, especially when we have not been seeking them. Re-orientating brings reflection on the terrain around us in a new way, opening up aspects we have not considered before.

As we allow our mindset to soften and our creativity to roam, not much may seem to be happening, but the re-orientating process can be both profound and transformational. It involves a shift of attention from outer events to our inner response, enabling us to focus on what we can change rather than what we cannot. From this, new insights and choices may emerge from the most unexpected places.

The psychiatrist Viktor Frankl's book *Man's Search for Meaning* explores his discovery of the indestructibility of choice in extremis. Thrown into a Nazi death camp during the Second World War, he noticed how his fellow-prisoners responded in different ways to the physical and psychological suffering they shared. Frankl recalls 'the men who walked through the huts comforting others, giving away their last piece of bread. They may have been few in number, but they offer sufficient proof that everything can be taken from a man but one thing: the last of the human freedoms — to choose one's attitude in any given set of circumstances, to choose one's own way.'

Another element of the re-orientating process is a new awareness of the bigger picture. We may realise that not only does our immediate problem go back further than we assumed, it also highlights much deeper issues. What we took as the whole story turns out to be only a part of it. For many, the unwanted journey of Covid-19 precipitated such re-orientating. The pandemic became a catalyst for exposing underlying issues that were around long before lockdown, particularly in the areas of work and relationships.

Re-orientating may involve the parent with difficulty setting boundaries for a child realising how hard it is to say an assertive 'no', even in their adult relationships; the partner seeking to stay in a difficult relationship, wondering whether they really want to be with this person — or just fear being alone; the loyal employee off sick with burn-out, reassessing to what extent their identity has been defined by their job. We need space to reflect on these matters without the urgency of immediate answers or action. As we re-orientate, we are opening up the ground for further movement at the right time.

Many times, I have sat as a counsellor alongside clients in the gentle process of re-orientating. It perhaps an under-sung dynamic of an unwanted journey, precisely because of its tentative, exploratory and reflective nature; yet, it is a process that resonates with many I have spoken with on such a journey.

I have already mentioned how, in the earlier times of our trying to start a family, each monthly disappointment was succeeded by my picking myself up and re-calculating a new timing for the same outcome. A sorrowful reckoning with the reality that I was going round and round in an unchanging loop eventually brought me to a re-orientating process, and a willingness to widen my horizons. A big shift came as I began to see leaving my current job and becoming pregnant as separate issues. This opened up a gap where something different could happen. It led me to reflect on wider questions about who, and where, I wanted to be, beyond parenting a child.

I pondered how much I wanted a teaching career, whether to pursue promotion and move school or stay put, where I was happy but potentially stuck in the cycle of more of the same. But re-orientating led me to consider another option: going part-time and opening up space for something new. This is what I eventually did, with the idea of starting writing. Just as I committed to this, an opportunity came up to write a column for the Bucks Free Press. The change brought fresh wind to my sails.

Taking time to re-orientate was a turning point, freeing me from assumptions to which I had become attached. I felt as though I had found a gap in a hedge I had walked past many times without noticing; a hidden opportunity to push through to a different space.

It may take only a relatively minor outer event to ignite an inner shift of mind-set, if it becomes that defining moment when 'enough is enough'. The Consultant's refusal of my request for surgery in that fateful arthritis consultation in a nondescript hospital side-room one rainy Monday afternoon was one such event. The next day, I used my journal for some free-writing about the anger and frustration I felt. Relocating my emotions onto the page removed some of the blocks to gaining a wider perspective. From here, I started to write lists of things I *could* do, giving myself permission to write freely, with nothing left off the table. As I re-read my lists of what I was still able to do, as well as what I could take on to improve things, I regained some energy, equilibrium and a sense of control.

I began to feel more settled as I resolved to pay more attention to looking after myself, rather than looking to surgery as a fix-all. I started to focus on simplifying my life, re-adjusting my pace of activity; re-balancing my diet, exercise and rest; and exploring the possibilities of alternative healthy approaches to well-being — from supplements to acupuncture. Since we make changes more effectively if we keep track of how we are doing, I recorded the steps I was taking, noting any impact these had on my joints and overall well-being. My circle of awareness began to widen. I found myself more observant of those around me, mindful of those managing mobility issues, and marvelling at the ease with which those with healthy bodies could move. I reflected on the assumptions I had been making about perfect health always being recoverable, and on how I generally responded when faced with problems I could not fix, only manage.

In her memoir of grieving, *H is for Hawk*, Helen MacDonald writes: 'There is a time in life when you expect the world to be always full of new things. And then comes a day when you realise that is not how it will be at all. You see that life will become a thing made of holes. Absences. Losses. Things that were there and are no longer. And you realise, too, that you have to grow around and between the gaps.'

Gaps and limits need not be preventers of growth but can actually promote it. They invite us to find a new way; but we need to take up the invitation and engage in the process. Writing can help slow us down to re-orientate, be open to insights and perspectives we had not previously considered, to become familiar with this terrain, and the secret, but significant, choices it may reveal.

Where to write

I have occasionally done a group writing exercise that invites everyone to imagine they have a year to write in any location they wish. Where would they go? What would they imagine as their ideal writing space? As we compare notes, common themes emerge.

Typically, there is a longing for a cosy room by a window that overlooks some beautiful aspect of the natural world — a forest, mountain range or the sea. This room with a view may be a writer's dream setting, but we need to find the practical places where we can write day by day. Fortunately, just as we can write at any time, we can also write in different locations.

The closest achievable space to the imagined cosy room may be a favourite spot at home. This is the writer Virginia Woolf's *Room of One's Own*; or at least, a room where one is on one's own. You may find you can settle here and be at home to yourself as you write. But this is not everyone's preferred place. As well as running the risk of interruption by a family member, we can easily become distracted by the '*I'll just...*' temptations: 'I'll just put out the washing', 'pick up the post', and so on. Wherever we choose to write, it needs to be somewhere we can concentrate.

Writing in a public space can, paradoxically, be a private experience. The local coffee shop can be an appealing place to journal. As you sit in the warm at your own table, the background buzz of coffee machines and conversation makes no demands on your personal time or attention. Some journallers have told me how they enjoy writing on a train journey, or even at the hairdresser's.

Journalling out and about includes writing outdoors. Some go for country walk with a small notebook. They may stop to make brief notes on their thoughts or what they notice around themselves, to transfer to their main journal back at home later. This approach combines the therapeutic benefits of writing with being close to nature, in the open air. It can also help to shift our perspective: our big concerns can shrink under a magnificent sky.

Writing alongside others may help you sustain the journalling habit. Writing is often a solitary pursuit; being part of a group can offer solidarity amongst the like-minded. You can share the experience of journalling without having to disclose the content. The Covid lockdown saw the growth of shared silent writing groups on Zoom, with many still flourishing, e.g. Shut up and Write and The Writers' Hour. Writing in a digital room may hold the balance for you between privacy and a mutually supportive connection with other writers.

Where we put ourselves as we write is one thing; where we put our words is another.

Would you rather journal onto paper or screen? Although this book assumes the writer is using pen and paper, there are no absolute rights and wrongs about best practice; both approaches have their advantages and drawbacks.

Many of us type faster than we can write, making keyboard journalling more conducive to an unimpeded flow of words. It can also help those who find it physically painful to write by hand. On-screen journals will always be legible, and it is easier to do a search through past entries. There are a range of apps that support different ways of structuring a journal, among them, Day One, Diarly, Diarium and Grid Diary.

If you feel you already spend too much time in front of a screen, you may prefer journalling with a pen. Writing at speed may not even be desirable; perhaps you want to journal more slowly and reflectively, away from the Internet's many distractions.

Writing physically absorbs our attention more fully, as both mind and body are engaged. We may also feel more connected with our words, and research indicates that we remember more of what we write than what we type. Writing by hand may also offer material for reflection, with its shape, legibility, size or direction varying depending on our state of mind.

Paper journallers have choices about whether to write on lined, blank or squared paper. Writing on blank paper can be particularly revealing, as well as lending itself more easily to other creative possibilities in filling the page. Some people head to their favourite stationery shop in town or online, to choose their journal with great care; they see this book as a special space that holds the precious material of their life's journey. They may write in it at a regular time, in a designated space and with a particular pen. Others opt for a simple exercise book, which enables them to write freely, without worrying about having to be perfectly neat and tidy. They may also feel more relaxed about carrying the book around with them and risking the odd scuffed edge or stain.

The final 'where' is where to keep your writing. It is important to find a place you are confident will remain private. If you are anxious that your writing might be found and read by others, it becomes difficult to trust yourself to be fully honest on page or screen. A journal on a computer file needs to be password-protected — and perhaps given an alias file name. Some paper journallers have tried to find less obvious hiding places by using their car's glove compartment or even an empty frozen-pea bag in their freezer! The ultimate location that ensures your writing is seen by no-one else is in the shredder.

You may wish to destroy writing that has helped you work through a challenging time. These words have fulfilled their purpose. Sending them on their way can be an expression of your freedom to let go of the past and move into a new season.

So, now it is over to you to explore where you will write — both the instruments you use and your physical location. Experiment with writing in various places, indoors and out, in solitude or with others around. Write your reflections on how writing in different settings impacts you. Does where you write change how and what you write in any way? What patterns of journal-writing do you want to establish in the light of what you discover?

Amy's Story: Writing Outdoors

Amy is a Secondary School Counsellor. Some of the young people she works with struggle to verbalise their feelings. Amy often suggests that they use the writing process to help them. It is something she says she has always done for herself. She has used it to support herself through the challenging journey of secondary infertility (having had two daughters from a previous relationship); a journey that has been ongoing for three years.

For Amy, exploring a deeply personal issue through talking onto the page in private has been especially helpful: 'Writing helped me process my feelings, as this was something I rather kept to myself.'

She finds that writing enables her to express the negatives of her experience. During her struggles with infertility, she turned instinctively to poetry, a form with a natural capacity to express and contain emotional intensity. 'Sometimes the writing expressed aspects of my IVF treatment in an obvious way,' she says. 'Sometimes it was a bit more hidden.'

Amy writes both indoors at home and outside, down at the beach. The beach was a go-to place of sanctuary when she was writing through particularly difficult times, such as after a negative pregnancy test result.

'I could be filled with so many mixed feelings,' she says, 'lots of them irrational. Writing helped to get them out of my head and on to paper, and they usually flowed out into a poem. It released the energy that I needed to express, and once it was out I always felt calmer and perhaps a little lighter, too.'

Amy keeps the poems that she has written, 'raw and untouched'. She says she may, at a later date, return to them to edit and assemble them as a poetry collection.

Amy would 'definitely encourage' anyone struggling with an issue to write about it: 'The writing can be in whatever form you want it to take and can be kept just for you if you wish.'

Amy's poem *The Whispers of the Sea* was written on the day of the negative pregnancy test result. 'I was on my own, as my partner was away. I knew I needed to be at the coast, so I got dressed, packed a few drinks and snacks and just drove there. I actually wrote in the sand along the seashore. Then I found a place to sit down and wrote a poem straight on to my phone.

'I don't like to go back to these pieces, as they are what I needed to write at the time. To me, it's more about expressing my emotions than having a perfect poem — whatever that may be. Afterwards, I was still devastated, but I felt better for putting some of my feelings into words.'

Below is Amy's poem:

The Whispers of the Sea

She writes in the sand with a pebble
"Why couldn't you have stayed with me?
Goodbye."
Then walks down to meet the sea
But the sea meets her first.
She watches as the waves cover her painted toes
And her feet sink into the muddy sand
She walks out into the sea
It's whispering to her to go deeper
Knee deep
Waist deep
Chest deep
Until she is finally submerged.
Then she comes up for air
Remembering how to breathe.

In the Re-orientating process, writing may help you to:

- Be content with just the next step
- Gain insight and courage for action
- Focus on choices you can make
- Plot and track a new course
- Find ways to widen the range of your journalling
- Turn from expectation to receptivity
- Free yourself of old approaches
- Play with new possibilities

Journalling Suggestions

> Be content with just the next step

The First Time I…

There was a first time for many things we now take in our stride or have moved beyond; a time when we had to take an initial step into a new experience. Somehow, we found a way of negotiating it, coming through and even flourishing in the wake of what might have been a daunting prospect.

Re-visiting a first-time activity in words can be powerful. When we enter unfamiliar territory, we are alert and alive to every moment, so our 'firsts' often create vivid memories. Journalling can be a way of recapturing what we sensed, thought and felt as we broke fresh ground in a new direction.

Think back to some firsts in your life. A few possibilities might be:

* Started at a new school
* Travelled by train or plane
* Got lost, or thought I was
* Moved house
* Drove a car

* Saw/went to sea
* Had an accident/broke a bone
* Went away without my parents
* Started work
* Experienced death

Choose one of these or something else that is a landmark-first for you. Take a few moments to settle yourself and bring that experience to mind. When you are ready, write about this 'first'. Describe it in as much sensory detail as you can. What did you see, hear, smell, etc.? Write about how you felt, both emotionally and physically. What were your thoughts? How did the experience unfold?

Afterwards, re-read what you have written from the perspective of the here and now, and reflect on the following questions:

- How does it feel to look back on this moment?
- What different steps were involved along the way?

- How did you know what to do next, even if you had not done it before?
- Where are you in relation to that experience now?
- What did you learn?
- Are there any useful insights here for your current situation?
- How do feel about the way you engaged with your 'first'?

> Gain insight and courage for action

Turning Points

As the re-orientating process involves a shift of position and a willingness to approach things from a new angle, it already has the potential to be a significant turning point. Our confidence as we go through this process can be strengthened as we explore how we have made other turning points in our lives before.

Draw a line to represent your life's course and note along it some key turning points on the way. (If you prefer to draw a line like a meandering river rather than a straight road, you may wish to jot down a few of the turning points first, so you can map them out as your river bends.) Your turning points are those moments that are most significant to you, from any area of life — relationships, education or work, achievements, health, creativity, interests — to your own attitude to yourself and the world. In what areas have you made the most important turning points?

Now choose one or two to explore in more detail. As you write about them, include:

- What led up to the turning point?
- What turned at the turning point — e.g. situation, inner motivation, personal action?
- What was turning point's outcome?
- What did you discover that could help you now, in this season of a new turning point?
- Does any of this writing suggest an immediate next step you could usefully take in your current situation?

> Focus on choices you *can* make

Duo of Lists

Writing sets of lists can also help you gain insight. They may be lists that directly oppose one another; for instance, making a decision may be helped by writing down a list of costs or losses involved, and then a list of benefits and gains. Writing down our reflections as we re read these lists may help us clarify our issues and resolve the matter.

One list may also *emerge from* another. For example, divide your page into two columns. Head one '**If only I could…**' and the other, '**But I can…**' List as many items as you can under those two headings. The list may emerge as a series of paired, contrasting statements.

What new possibilities and perspectives does this writing release? Re-read what you have written and note down any observations that strike you as particularly important.

Equally, one list may lead to another. For example, a list of ambitious, longer-term goals may lead to further *lists* that break down these aims into specific, smaller steps you could take towards achieving them. You may need, however, to cross a few items off that first list to make the later list(s) practical.

> Plot and track new courses

Writing Modes for Decision-Making

A good decision involves assembling facts, creating possibilities, weighing up implications and factoring-in feelings. These four aspects relate to four writing modes: descriptive, intuitive, reflective and cathartic. Because some come more naturally to us than others, it can be useful to explore an issue by approaching it in each writing mode separately, to ensure all bases are covered, and then synthesising the insights that emerge.

Choose an issue or a decision you are facing; perhaps there is an aspect of your life that feels stuck and you want to explore a new direction. Take the writing modes in turn and write for up to ten minutes on each one.

- In **Descriptive Mode**, write about the issue or situation as precisely and informatively as you can. Be a neutral observer and chart the facts.

Rely on what your senses are telling you, without judgement.

- In **Intuitive Mode**, do some free-writing, either continuously or as a list or mind map (to create a mind map, write the issue in the middle of your blank page and branch out from the centre with lines that link associated words and ideas).
Brainstorm as many creative possibilities as you can. Let yourself be imaginative, even inventive, without censoring or judging what comes up.
- In **Reflective Mode**, assess the viability of your options. What are the consequences and implications of following them through? What might be the challenges, opportunities and longer-term outcomes?
- In **Cathartic Mode**, tune into your feelings about the issue generally and any emotions that have surfaced during this exercise. Write these down honestly, directly and from the heart. Where might others' feelings also need to be factored?

Read what you have written, to review these different strands. Write a few sentences about what you notice and where this takes you. Which mode did you find most difficult and which came most naturally? (Noting this might highlight a blind spot in your decision-making.) Do these modes point to a particular action or response? Is this what you anticipated or has it surprised you?

This whole mode-writing exercise could be completed as a form of mind map: divide your page into four squares, label each one and jot down your ideas for the four modes in note form.

Look over these notes and add some summarising sentences about any conclusions you can make, as you draw together the different things you have written.

Poetry Exploration

> Find ways to widen the range of your journalling

Diary

A century ago
last year before you left

someone gave me a diary
which I didn't need
to write down the hours
I spent with you
there is no need
to write happiness
and now when I come to read
the pages are all blank
I put away a book
as empty as the year was full
if someone should find it and look
it would seem as if the year had passed
leaving no trace — an uneventful year
but my heart is scarred with bitter pains
nothing has been recorded
but I know however old I live to be
however many pages I fill with words
only those empty pages will move me.

Diary was written by a fellow pupil at my secondary school. It was one of a sequence read out in a play celebrating our school's 50th anniversary. As a backstage helper, I heard this poem at every performance. I found it haunting and it has stayed with me ever since.

In a re-orientation process, we can find ourselves seeing what faces us from a new angle. This poem helps us look at how we approach the issue of balance in journal-writing. There is the balance of content. How do you respond to the assertion that 'there is no need/to write happiness'? The implication is that we only write when times are tough. Is this the case for you? Write some reflective sentences on what might be valuable to you in writing through both good and challenging times. Is there a bias towards one or the other in your own journal? Do you want to make any changes?

If writing takes us away from being active in the outside world, how do we balance this with times of stepping back to record and reflect? To what extent is it a case of either/or? Can one enrich the other? Write about how this dynamic works out for you and reflect on anything you may wish to re-adjust.

The poem's direct and accessible language expresses intense feeling. Line follows line, with no punctuation, in a continuous outpouring of spontaneous emotion.

Experiment with putting into words something you feel strongly about, using the poem's form: short, free-verse lines, all in lower case and without punctuation. Write continuously but do not rush. Try to match the poem's length of approximately 20 lines, so you encapsulate essentials rather than become overwhelmed by detail. How does it feel to express something strongly in this focussed way?

> Turn from expectation to receptivity

Come new to this day

     Spit out the
sour taste of unmet expectation.

Arrive curious

From *Prescription For the Disillusioned*

Rebekah del Rio

As we re-orientate, we start opening up to ways forward other than those hoped for. This is a tender turning point to navigate. Writing can help us clarify its particular challenges and move us through.

We may bristle at a poem called *Prescription For the Disillusioned*, but its opening word 'Come' breathes invitation rather than instruction. By offering such a 'prescription', this poem encourages us that 'disillusionment' is not the end. We are invited to let go, not only of former plans, but also the results we anticipated. You can read the whole poem at the poet's website, *rebekahdelriopoetry.com*.

Experience, knowledge and belief can be our allies, but at this juncture they have become too rigid to help us. The hard, old ground needs to be broken up for something new to grow. Even the shape of our life's stories needs to be released so that the narratives we tell ourselves can be reformulated. (It has been said that one way we know things are different for us is when our stories have changed.)

The Speaker's call to 'Spit out the/sour taste of unmet expectation' is a powerful phrase that highlights that most stark sense of disillusionment.

Write a sentence or two to put this into your own words. Now dive a little deeper. Can you identify what has fuelled that expectation? It might be a belief you hold about how life should be. It might be the strength of your desire, or something you've been told, or an experience — your own or others' — that has set a precedent for your assumptions. Write a few sentences to define these as best you can.

Elsewhere in the poem, the Speaker imagines our experience and our plans weighing us down like a stiff coat or suit of armour. What would it be like to take these off? Would you be left feeling liberated? Or exposed? Vulnerable? Cold?

If you were going to re-clothe yourself with a lightweight garment of curiosity, what would you be wearing?

Set the intention to walk through the day in this garment, ready to be receptive to new experiences and respond to whatever comes your way. At the day's end, write some reflections on how this has worked out. What new things have you seen, even wondered at? What fresh fragrances have drifted your way as you have breathed in today's fresh air?

> Free yourself of old approaches

Perhaps It Would Eventually Erode, But…

That rock that we
have been pushing up
the hill — that one

that keeps rolling back down
and we keep pushing
back up — what if

we stopped? We are not
Sisyphus. This rock
is not a punishment.

It's something we've chosen
to push. Who knows why.
I look at all the names

we once carved into
its sedimentary sides.
How important

I thought they were,
those names. How
I've clung to labels,

who's right, who's wrong,
how I've cared about
who's pushed harder

and who's been slack.
Now all I want
is to let the rock

roll back to where it belongs,
which is wherever it lands,
and you and I could,

imagine!, walk unencumbered,
all the way to the top and
walk and walk and never stop

except to discover what
our hands might do
if for once they were

receiving.

Rosemerry Wahtola Trommer

This poem draws on Greek myth, where deceitful King Sisyphus is punished in the underworld by being forced to push a boulder up a steep hill — only for it to keep rolling back down as he reaches the top. Elements of myths can touch on universal experience, and this poem explores the story's imagery of fruitless and wearying labour.

A re-orientating process can be a time to evaluate habitual ways of doing things. Perhaps you, like the poem's Speaker, want to adjust some approaches to your life's concerns as you start to see them in a different way.

If you are feeling exhausted by wasted effort, you are not alone. The poem's stone-shifters are plural, with the Speaker calling out the rock as 'something we've chosen/to push'. What rock have you been repeatedly pushing up a slope, perhaps on your own, perhaps with others?

Write about this rock, describing what it is and who else may be involved in the gravity-defying attempt to move it. What once-so-important names — or perhaps even old inscriptions — are carved into this rock? What labels have you held onto — perhaps for self as well as others, and what judgements have you made about others' involvement in this frustrating project?

The Speaker wants to leave the rock to its own devices and move forward with a new freedom and receptivity. Write about what you want to do with your rock; what would that look like in practical terms? You may want to look for a real stone to pick up and put aside, as a way of marking your intentions about what you want to leave behind.

> Play with new possibilities

Brooklyn Bridge

12.17am and cyclists still ride by.

In the nightlife's ebb and flow
on Brooklyn Bridge balanced
between the past and present in me

I know the bridges I have toppled from
the hands that didn't break my fall
and the faith in me it takes
to step and step across the sky.

Above the steel water's stare
pressed into the night

light after light
burns my black bright.

Francesca Pridham

New York's Brooklyn Bridge links Manhattan and Brooklyn across the East River. This tourist landmark is particularly dramatic to walk across at night. In this poem, the Speaker stands at the brink of doing just that. It will be no brief dash: the pedestrian promenade is over a mile long.

A bridge is a passageway over a potentially dangerous obstacle between two areas of solid ground. Stepping onto any such construction can bring up our awareness of the risk, excitement and possibilities of making a transition.

There is a frisson in the air as the Speaker stands poised to step out. Their sense of vulnerability reminds them of times when they were unsupported as they failed to reach the other side. Do memories of others letting you down make you reluctant to take risks? What bridges have you toppled off that have dented your confidence? Write about how these experiences have impacted you.

Now, come to stand with the Speaker at Brooklyn Bridge (you may wish to find an image of it online). Describe what you see around and ahead of you. What is inviting and what is threatening? Write about how you feel at the prospect of crossing this bridge.

Taking a deep breath, you step onto the bridge. What inner resources can you find to help you? Note any pulse of faith, hope, courage or desire that can stir you onwards, however faint.

There are external factors to help you, too, in the form of the pinprick line of lights across the open walk-way. It is said that across the river, the sparkling Manhattan skyline draws the walker on like a moth to a flame. What lights are guiding you as you 'step and step across the sky'? Write about these and how they affect you.

After these first steps, imagine you keep walking. Write about what happens next.

When you find yourself…	Writing may help you to…
• Willing to adapt to new parameters	• Be content with the next step
• Starting to explore a changed world	• Gain insight and courage for action
• Looking for what one can, not cannot, do	• Focus on choices you *can* make
• Asking many questions — with few answers	• Plot and track a new course
• Adrift among unexpected possibilities	• Find ways to re-balance writing for support
• Living with uncertainty of outcome	• Turn from expectation or receptivity
• Loosening loyalty to an outdated story	• Free yourself of old approaches
• Opening up to new knowledge	• Play with new possibilities

Chapter 5: Resourcing

- More effective at self-care
- More open and vulnerable
- Incorporating new ways forward
- Managing emotions better
- Discovering surprising new avenues
- Regaining identity beyond your issue
- Valuing well-being in the now
- Reconnecting with those around us

The sun streams through the floor-to-ceiling windows that form a wall in this room in Maggie's Cancer Care Centre, Merseyside. Outside is a newly ploughed field. Inside, the group sits in silence at a long table. Eight heads are bent down; eight pens move across eight pages. The Creative Writing session is underway.

Writing is one of various therapeutic activities offered at Maggie's Cancer Centres across the UK as part of their programme of information and support. The charity enables those affected by cancer to make positive choices in their own care, as they navigate their way through medical treatment.

Running these writing sessions soon became the highlight of my week, but I had some trepidation at the outset. I decided to face the issue that most concerned me and ask the group directly, 'Do you want to write about your cancer?'

'No, we don't,' said one participant, immediately. 'It will come into the writing anyway. It just helps to know that this is a safe place for that to happen.'

Another felt the benefit of writing activities that were creative, rather than specifically expressive about the illness. 'I felt I needed to be here,' she said. 'I was becoming very stale and locked-in on myself. After the first few pieces of writing, I found my horizons widening again.'

Creative writing offered this patient a fresh focus; it released her to reconnect with the world beyond her challenging circumstances. She began to feel better in herself, more energised and with a new perspective. She still had her situation, but it did not *have her* in the same way. Sometimes we are 'resourced' most powerfully when we become absorbed in something that releases our attention from its most pressing claim.

Several participants remarked on the pleasure and satisfaction of discovering what they could create in words: one wrote a delightful alphabet poem about dogs (with a different dog breed for almost every letter). Writing helped them keep hold of their identity, independent of hospital corridors and appointments. As writer Sheridan Voysey observed: 'A greater tragedy than a broken dream is a life forever defined by it.'

We wrote about many aspects of our lives: our origins, passions, life-experiences and places special to us. We read our writing to one another; practised using all our senses to pay attention to the present moment and chosen memories, and then putting words to what we noticed.

These sessions highlighted an essential element of the resourcing process: making connections. Connecting is risky. We may feel vulnerable as we open up, without and within. Our instinct in tough times is often to cocoon ourselves in self-protection rather than reach out. It is important, of course, to take time to rest and renew, but we also need the resourcing that comes from opening up. Permanent withdrawal starves us of this nourishment.

The resourcing process is about finding the fuel to sustain us on our way. This may involve trying activities and approaches we have not considered before. One of these may be writing. Most of those who joined the creative writing group at Maggie's were not seasoned writers. They summoned the courage to try something new, and most discovered how creative and expressive writing could support their well-being. This was not the case for all, but the exploratory nature of the resourcing process also includes letting go of what is not working for us.

Writing together means not just connecting with our words on the page, but also with those around us. This counters the aloneness that can lead to isolation and depression. As those at the Maggie's Centre found, being alongside others in similar situations can offer the support of a shared understanding that does not necessarily have to be spoken.

Connecting beyond the circle of our fellow-travellers is also important, helping us to remain part of the mix of life around us. At times we may need to go gently, as tender areas may be exposed or misunderstood. During my difficult days with infertility, I remember on one occasion being taken to a newly formed women's group. As we introduced ourselves, each woman started with her name and the details of her children. I dreaded my turn. Just before me, the friend who had brought me kindly introduced herself differently. But the possibilities of an uncomfortable moment was the risk I took if I wanted to be in company where my loss was hidden.

Then there were the advice-givers: 'Have you thought of…?' followed by some practical suggestion or piece of information which would solve our infertility — usually something I already knew. I had to learn not to be too harsh on those who wanted to help. Their motives were good, even if their offering inappropriate.

It was not fixers but trusted friends who proved to be the most precious resource; friends who would listen, often to the same feelings and stories over and over again. They offered their presence, empathy and sometimes practical help.

At one stage, we were having similar infertility treatment to a couple we knew. Ours failed; theirs worked out. I felt devastated. When I told a close friend what had happened, she simply held me in a hug and said, 'That must have been so difficult for you.' It was all I needed. Pain truly heard was somehow released.

Connecting to the environment can also be part of our resourcing. The therapeutic benefits of getting out into the fresh air, particularly in natural surroundings, has become more appreciated by people during and since the pandemic. Nature can be a source of solace, inspiring both poets and scientists alike. And if mobility is an issue, take heart: research published by the Vrije University Medical Centre in the Netherlands has found that even looking at photographs of nature provides sufficient stimulus to lower stress levels. I have also increasingly found it helpful to place natural objects around the home: a vase of flowers, a shell, or a small stone.

The resourcing process can also involve seeking to make a connection with the bigger picture. Hard journeys raise challenging questions about the direction of our lives. When old ways of being are turned upside down, former certainties and assumptions are shaken out. We find ourselves reassessing what really matters as we feel for a purposeful way to walk through our loss.

Drawing some meaning out of our situation helps sustain our path through it, but it is something we need to discover and own for ourselves. Our understanding must hold personal meaning for us, not be another's imposed template. Resourcing can lead us to explore the defining values and deepest desires we choose as guides. Existing beliefs can be tested and faith honed or even awakened in a shifting of spiritual ground.

As my prayers for a child went unanswered, I began to re-examine my own Christian faith: was it a formula for wish-fulfilment? Did the absence of children mean I had done something wrong? Was God even there? Over time and talk, in seeking and silence, through disappointment and discovery, I eventually emerged — after a long and bumpy ride — with a more securely grounded but open-ended faith in a God who insists on living outside the boxes of my assumptions.

Whether in connecting more deeply to ourselves, to others, to our environment or to the bigger picture, the resourcing process is one of active engagement; we open up to what is authentic, has substance and is worth its weight in the gold it can bring to our lives. We are looking for what will sustain us, more than merely entertain us.

However, this does not mean the process cannot be playful. We are free to investigate and experiment with what might help: to pursue a course or put it aside; to develop a different way of being; to 'unlearn' as well as learn; to find what works for us by trial and error. This can be a time to engage creativity, curiosity, adaptability and a sense of discovery.

Looking for what can support us where we are now is an opportunity for active choice within the constraint of our circumstances. This in itself can soothe stress and re-awaken our energy.

Bernie Seigel's book *Love, Medicine and Miracles* explores factors that improve the odds of a cancer patient's survival. He writes of how when a diagnosis was given, some patients would simply go home and give up; some would ask for treatment to be carried out, while remaining passive. But a third group would ask what they could do to contribute towards their healing. This active group tended to make better progress. They used diagnosis not as an end point but as a turning point.

There are many potential resources around us: people and activities; time, place and space; information and education; input and reflection. They may be physical, spiritual, material, social, psychological, or creative. Amongst such an array, writing is a resource available to us freely as a support that we can pick up 24/7, with a wide range of ways we can go about it.

How to write

One of my personal pleasures is cooking a risotto on a Saturday evening. Ingredients vary according to the recipe, stock cupboard, taste and occasion — though have you noticed how even when two people follow one particular recipe, the resulting dish is never quite the same? We will be re-visiting making risotto in a poem later in this chapter.

As with risotto, there is no one bespoke recipe for journal-writing. Each journal has a unique flavour from its particular mix of ingredients. We choose not only what, but how, we want to write, using techniques appropriate to the purpose of our writing at the time.

How we approach the page is the first factor. My Saturday night risotto cooking is enhanced by some personal rituals: turning on the radio; pouring that first twilight glass of wine; watching over the pan in readiness to add more stock. In the same way, our writing times can be framed with rituals we find meaningful and supportive. These might include lighting a candle, brewing a fresh coffee, turning our phone to silent, smoothing our page or positioning the laptop.

As we prepare to write, we settle ourselves and take a few deep breaths, consciously bringing our senses into the present moment. We can sharpen such 'noticing' on paper with a sensory check-in, jotting down briefly what we can see, hear, smell, touch and perhaps even taste. We may take a moment for an emotional check-in by noting down three words that sum up how we feel right now. There are various approaches we can take as we start to write.

We have already noted how very structured forms at one end of the writing spectrum contrast with completely free-flow writing at the other. Perhaps you need to express an emotion, explore an issue, or get to the bottom of something that is bothering you — even if you are not quite sure what that is. Free-writing may be the way forward here, as you let your writing take you where it wants to go.

Free-writing can also help with whatever may be pre-occupying your thoughts, moving them out of your head into the separate space of the page. Just remember to set those boundaries of time or space around such writing, to ensure you emerge in a better place on the other side. It can act as a release from an emotional or mental straitjacket.

At other times, structure might be what you need most. Where life feels chaotic or its demands overwhelming, some sort of order is required. Making a list or creating a mind map can be an accessible starting point. Once your swirling concerns are pinned down in words, they can be worked with. They can be grouped or ordered, prioritised or dismissed. One or two can be selected from the mix for particular attention, perhaps through further writing or identifying some action you can take.

You may want to write to capture a special moment or occasion, from a planned event to an unexpected incident or conversation that feels highly significant. Here, your writing will focus on the vivid sensory and emotional details that re-evoke your experience. Your tone may be celebratory or more reflective as you explore what makes this incident or event so important to you today.

How you write can be as creative — and as experimental — as you like. When emotion is intense, you may find you naturally gravitate towards poetry as the best way to distill and arrange your feelings. Expressing yourself in poetic form can help you honour what matters to you with its own shape and beauty.

Such creativity can be playful, too. Changing your writing genre can release new insights and bring a valuable shift of perspective. Journallers I know have sometimes enjoyed exploring a personal dilemma or challenge by writing about it as if it were a fairytale. Re-imagining their situation in this form has helped them explore it in a different way and with a lighter touch.

Another way of writing to help you shift your perspective is to change point of view. Writing about yourself in the third person ('he/she/they') rather than the first person ('I'), creates a little distance. This can foster a more objective perspective, as well as making it more possible to explore an issue that feels too raw to engage in close-up.

You can also experiment with changing your emotional slant. If you wished you felt more hopeful about a situation, ask yourself what would be different if you were, and try writing from that angle. You are not forcing yourself to be hopeful, simply trying on an attitude for size and opening up a new possibility.

We can write not just as we wish but as *anyone* we wish. This is useful if you are writing to explore some particular interaction or relationship. If you have an issue with someone, or simply find them very trying, try writing about things as if you were them. This is an opportunity to cultivate empathy — alongside a splash of imagination; it can start to change you, whatever may or not happen elsewhere.

Where we need to find our voice in relationship with someone else, we can write an unsent letter (with the emphasis on *unsent*), to express exactly what we want to say. Putting our writing into the form of a dialogue can be a way to explore a relationship in general or to rehearse a potentially difficult conversation in particular.

Then, there are those internal conversations that we have going on between different parts of ourselves. Giving voice to two conflicting internal aspects by writing them as a dialogue may help us listen to what each may have to say and needs to hear. It can bring a deeper understanding, and peace, to warring parts of us, helping us manage our whole personality.

Finally, there is how we put words on the page. Do you want to write slowly, reflectively, listening for what is coming up? Or quickly and uncritically, from the gut, to cheat any self-censoring? Do you want to leave plenty of space at the margins and between paragraphs? How mindful do you want to be of spelling, punctuation, legibility, etc., for ease of reading back later?

Of the techniques and approaches available, which are you drawn to most? Write some reflections on how you want to write, challenging yourself to explore a way of writing that has little immediate appeal. It can be surprisingly fruitful to write outside your comfort zone; you do not have to do so all the time. You can develop your unique recipe of writing methods, adjusting them as and when needed, as you find your own voice on the page.

Sheryl's Story: Writing to Find Her Voice

Sheryl's planned journey became diverted into a very much unwanted one. As she travelled through Asia en route to a life in Australia, the anti-malarial tablets she took as a precaution for a visit to Vietnam set off a severe allergic reaction. Sheryl developed 'horrendous pain' in her larynx and had to return to the UK. It was the start of a two-year trek through various hospitals, specialists and medications to get to the heart of the problem and find the help she needed.

She describes this as the hardest period of her life: 'I was near-suicidal and off work, unable to speak without pain and at a complete loss that my once healthy, happy self had gone. I still live with my condition and take high doses of pain killers, which affect my concentration and memory. I am grateful, however, to have found the right medication that allows me to talk without too much pain, and use writing and mindfulness to maintain my wellbeing.'

Sheryl struggled to accept the life-changing circumstances and devastation of ongoing, chronic pain. 'I was quite desperate. I binged on food to comfort myself: when I ate, I couldn't feel my pain and it filled me up emotionally in the short-term.' However, writing offered a more fruitful solace in processing her feelings. She says, while 'talking therapy helped, writing enabled me to go more directly and deeply into things'.

Writing allowed her to express herself more freely: '[It] became my voice to say what I really felt. I'd always enjoyed it and previously used poetry to process and reflect on things. I had also written a couple of plays. Writing felt like a natural place to start to help me heal.'

Sheryl wrote a mix of free-writing, journalling and poetry. She wrote whenever, and wherever, she needed to — in bed, at the kitchen table, in the garden and at different times of day. She also went on retreats and three years later, spent some months in Spain, where she wrote extensively around the landscape and her travelling experience.

She admits that initially her writing was 'all pretty negative'. 'At the time I only saw a black hole. Now I see things more positively on most days. I can see that this was life's way of changing things around to help me stay put and confront my anxieties rather than run away. Being ill gave me the anchor I needed to work with something that has been keeping me unhappy.'

Sheryl keeps everything she has written. 'I've recently moved house and now have all my notepads — from this period of ill-health and before — out on my bookshelf. They have been in boxes for years. It's nice to see them liberated. Perhaps it shows that I'm no longer ashamed and feel more accepting of myself.'

She is enthusiastic about the value of writing for everyone and anyone: 'Forget about rhyming couplets and Shakespeare. Your voice is just as beautiful and deserves to be let out. Your creativity is just waiting in the wings. Writing is your chance to express what cannot be spoken. It's a confidante and friend. The page contains and accepts all of you unconditionally. Words take you on a unique journey.'

Below is one of Sheryl's poems:

Summer

That summer, suitcases lined up like soldiers,
Full of expectations, escape, the dreamy hope of 'exit'
Words, clumsy and child-like, a lovely, honey coated authenticity but with a false taste,
Nested in my heart.

Alas!

My larynx became a silent cave, a conductor of muffled screams, childhood conversations,
A disembodied map of geographical markings illuminating 'why me?'
The certain smell of unfinished work.

My voice faded into a whisper,
Me, a passenger in a body
My old self distilled into sadness, dismantled piece by piece…
Only the lump remained and-
An all-pervasive homelessness
Forced to sit in the saddle.
A beat.
Silence.
Nothing to change the story.

In the Resourcing process, writing may help you to:

- Identify what is helpful
- Explore openness
- Generate new ideas and angles
- Work constructively with emotions
- Be receptive to fresh input
- Enjoy new avenues of creativity
- Receive the sustenance of the day
- Cherish and strengthen supportive connections

Journalling Suggestions

> Identify what is helpful

A Resource Review

Write a list of the things that have energised or nourished you in some way this week.

Set aside any thoughts about what these ought to be, or even what you intended to do you good. What has actually helped you along your way — however inconsequential or surprising it may seem?

Now, write a second list of the things that have drained you. Again, do not pre-judge what you think should be draining, write what *actually* has drained you.

Re-read what you have written and write a third list. Looking ahead, consider what might resource you over the next week. What changes could you make that will increase these things? What changes could you make to reduce what drains you? These can be small, do-able adjustments, such as spending a bit more time outdoors, or getting to bed a little earlier. Use your first two lists to suggest what you might put on the third.

You may wish to repeat this exercise over a few weeks, or even as a daily practice for a while. As you trace any emerging patterns, you can develop and fine-tune your resource list — your personal tool-box for own particular journey.

> Explore openness

Dare to be Different

Break a taboo. Make a list of things that you do not usually write or even talk about.

Choose one from your list and write a few sentences to express something you rarely put on the page. If you find you have more to write, keep going for a few sentences more.

Experiment with form. If you never write lists, unsent letters or dialogues, try your hand at one. If you always write in a very structured way, try some free-writing. Experiment with writing in poetic form, penning brief lines down the page.

Try writing with your other hand or in another colour. Turn the page sideways and write about something you want to see from a different angle.

There are many possibilities for having fun and doing something a bit different. You may have some more ideas of your own. Afterwards, take some moments to note down how it felt to try something new.

> Generate new ideas and angles

A Letter from Your Future Self

Writing enables us to become time-travellers. Looking at an issue from the vantage point of a different time can highlight what is really important, overcome blind spots and may even generate a fresh approach to a current situation.

Imagine yourself at the endpoint of the particular journey you are now on. How do you feel? What has changed for you and in you? Take some moments to imagine yourself in the place of 'after all this is over' —

whatever 'this' is. Pay attention to how you are, as well as how your circumstances have resolved.

Write a letter from your future to your current self. Write as a wise and kind friend. Tell your current self what it is like to be where you are, and offer advice and encouragement.

What has helped your future self reach this new place? How did you manage to find your way through? What advice do you have for your current self?

Re-read what you have written and note what most resonates. What insights does your future self have about how you are doing, or things you might try? Look at any adjustments or choices you want to make in the light of your future self's words.

This exercise is not intended as a magic formula for achieving a set goal; its aim is to elicit creative possibilities for how you might live more hopefully in your current life-situation.

> Work constructively with emotions

Writing through the Lens of...

Against the backdrop of evidence supporting the benefits of writing about life's difficulties, we have already noted writing researcher Megan Hayes' work on the value of writing 'through the lens' of positive emotion. This is not to pretend that everything in the garden is rosy. In this imaginative exercise, we import a chosen emotion into our current circumstances to discover how it might transform our outlook. If we were looking at our situation through the eyes of, say, love or hope, what might come to light? What would things look like and what might become significant?

Try this now: choose a positive emotion such as hope, love, joy, peace, compassion, forgiveness or simply curiosity. Take some moments to engage with how you experience that emotion. Where and how do you feel it? Is it accompanied by particular thought patterns or bodily sensations?

When you have captured a sense of your chosen emotion, write about your day or a situation you want to explore as if you were looking through its lens. How does this change what you notice and regard as important?

Poetry Exploration

> Be receptive to fresh input

Things I Learned Last Week

Ants, when they meet each other,
usually pass on the right.

Sometimes you can open a sticky
door with your elbow.

A man in Boston has dedicated himself
to telling about injustice.
For three thousand dollars he will
come to your town and tell you about it.

Schopenhauer was a pessimist but
he played the flute.

Yeats, Pound, and Eliot saw art as
growing from other art. They studied that.

If I ever die, I'd like it to be
in the evening. That way, I'll have
all the dark to go with me, and no one
will see how I begin to hobble along.

In The Pentagon one person's job is to
take pins out of towns, hills, and fields,
and then save the pins for later.

William Stafford

In this poem, the Speaker gathers together a week's worth of learning. If we are curious and attentive, without and within, we can open ourselves to much that is new, and gain both information and insight.

Our minds have the capacity to range freely from the trivial to the profound, and across seemingly unconnected subjects and thoughts. The poem captures this apparently random movement of attention as it collects the diverse input of an ordinary week. Of course, we are not neutral observers; we notice what is around us because it impacts us in some way, making some connection with who, where and how we are. Can we deduce anything about the Speaker from what has stayed with them from last week?

Reflect on your last week and make your own list of what you have learned. Think about things learned from direct experience as well as other sources. Incorporate facts and knowledge alongside perhaps personal realisations — as in the Speaker's reflection on their own death. Now, select from this list to create your own poem. Arrange your material in the order that you find most satisfying. This need not be chronological.

This exercise can be pleasurable as well as creative. You may wish to repeat it over several weeks, as a weekly review. You could also focus on other elements from your week, such as the things I… experienced, tried, said or wrote; the people I thought about and/or met.

> Enjoy new avenues of creativity

Risotto

I'd work from recipes, measure carefully, hover
anxiously. Be so bored by the craft and science
I'd then lose all interest in eating it.
So I cooked risotto every night for a month,
made it instinctive, natural, a simple habit,
as if I'd grown up in a red tiled Italian town
where emerald basil sprouts wildly in the gutters.

Rice, onion, garlic abandoned into hot butter
without a thought. Pepper. Bubbling white wine.
Stock, slipping from a jug, uncalculated.
Dared break the cardinal rule never to leave it.
Judged by eye. Knew by the soft heaving gloss
when to let saffron or prawns or asparagus
fall from my heedless hands. Got it so perfect

I can start from scratch, soon be piling plates,
like breathing, like walking, like humming Puccini,

as if another woman, olive eyed, laughing
like Sunday church bells all the while, has done it.

Mary Woodward

This poem celebrates the transformative movement from doing something by the book to practising an instinctive skill — like a shift from painting by numbers to a more naturally creative brush-stroke. What skills can you identify as part of your creative life? They may be culinary, or from a different field altogether.

The poem outlines the first steps of learning then progresses to a vivid, sensory evocation of full absorption with the creative task. The final triumphant lines celebrate the Speaker's ability to make risotto like a true Italian.

Write about a skill you have developed over time, perhaps with the same dedication evinced in the poem. Enjoy tracing in words the contrast between what you are able to do now but could not when you started. The Speaker became intentional about cooking risotto every night. What factors enabled you to move from awkward beginnings to the ease of experience?

We might also apply the poem's wisdom to wider life-skills. If we want to develop new ways of living, we need to start with intentional practices — however imperfect — that eventually settle into natural habits. What fresh approaches might you want to nurture in your daily living? A new way to be kind to yourself; to be creative; to change your outlook and the way you talk to yourself?

Break down your goal into a recipe of small steps. Write down the first ones you intend to make as you start to learn your chosen new skill.

> Receive the sustenance of the day

For The Sake Of Strangers

No matter what the grief, its weight,
we are obliged to carry it.
We rise and gather momentum, the dull strength
that pushes us through crowds.

And then the young boy gives me directions
so avidly. A woman holds the glass door open,
waits patiently for my empty body to pass through.
All day it continues, each kindness
reaching toward another – a stranger
singing to no one as I pass on the path, trees
offering their blossoms, a child
who lifts his almond eyes and smiles.
Somehow they always find me, seem even
to be waiting, determined to keep me
from myself, from the thing that calls to me
as it must have once called to them –
this temptation to step off the edge
and fall weightless, away from the world.

Dorianne Laux

This poem does not shirk grief's reality, with its temptation to turn away from the world, and perhaps even life itself. Yet, the Speaker also recognises the world drawing them back into its embrace through the unexpected kindnesses of strangers. Whether deliberate or unconscious, these gifts bring comfort. Nothing repairs the loss, but the Speaker's heart is gently opened to the consolations that can emerge over an ordinary day.

Can you discern times when a similar, positive dynamic seems to be flowing towards you? It might be in a direct, intended action; in something you notice happening; or in an encounter with the natural world that lifts you.

Write the line 'All day it continues' and underneath, create lines of your own list poem following Laux's model. You could start other lines with 'And then' or 'Somehow', as she has. Think about who or what is coming to meet your senses: friends, strangers, places, incidents, natural objects. Your list may range more widely than the poet's.

If 'All day it continues' feels too much of a stretch just now, adapt the line i.e.: 'And still it continues' or 'All week/month', or 'Over time it continues'.

Chapter 5: Resourcing

> Cherish and strengthen supportive connections

All Weathers

You've seen them, footprints in the snow
that trudge for miles together,
then drift apart
as we might have, or so I thought,
to seek out different weather.

And then you came back and you and you,
bearing cards, flowers,
winging e-mails.
Out of the blue you came as snow fell
and the road seemed lost,
to shore me up, rockfast.

Helen Hill

Other people are a significant resource in challenging times, though we cannot always predict how they will respond. Sometimes, those we assumed would be there for us when winter descends are nowhere to be seen, whilst unexpected others come right alongside. This can be disorientating, but it may be more about them than us. Some instinctively understand the landscape of loss; others are unsettled by it.

Cast adrift in life's winter, the poem's Speaker has few expectations of companionship. Yet the parting snow-prints of the first verse give way to the surprising arrival of supportive friends in the second. 'And then you came back,' says the poem, 'And you and you.' Write about three people who have supported you through some of your own life's rough weather. These may be friends, or perhaps those who emerged as friends through that time. How did they come to you and what gifts did they bring? What impact did they have on you and how does this feel?

Write a few sentences about what you find supportive in difficult times. What helps shore you up? Is it a material gift, like flowers? Kind words, spoken or sent? A listening ear or a practical action?

The resourcing process involves moving out from isolation to connection. Re-read what you have written about your three friends. Would they be aware of the things you have put on the page here? If not, could you find a way of letting them know — perhaps in a thank-you card, e-mail or even text? Write a note of gratitude and let them know what their support has meant to you.

When you find yourself…	Writing may help you to…
• More effective at self-care	• Identify what is helpful
• More open and vulnerable	• Explore openness
• Incorporating new ways forward	• Generate new ideas and angles
• Managing emotions better	• Work constructively with emotions
• Discovering surprising new avenues	• Be receptive to fresh input
• Regaining identity beyond your issues	• Enjoy new avenues of creativity
• Valuing well-being in the now	• Receive the sustenance of the day
• Reconnecting with those around us	• Cherish and strengthen supportive connections

Chapter 6: Re-energising

- Grounded in a new rhythm
- Knowing how to engage the territory
- Open to a new destination
- Having a greater capacity to adapt
- Recovering hope
- More able to overcome knock-backs
- With a re-located sense of purpose
- In a sustainable way of being

Resilience does not look or behave like a Superhero; you would be hard-pressed to identify her as having any special powers at all. She looks ordinary, even a little scruffy. Her sturdy walking shoes are worn down at heel, and there are patches on the knees of her jeans — but a quiet light and inner confidence gleams from her eyes. Her posture is erect. She walks with assurance. She is agile, patiently negotiating her way through the rocks on her path, picking herself up and dusting herself off whenever she stumbles. Turning obstacles into stepping stones seems to be her speciality. Resilience is lightfooted, but able to steady herself in the gusts of an oncoming wind, and through the long twilight of an exhausting day. She has a warm smile for everyone — even those who greet her with a frown or a snarl. She is an unassuming travelling companion; you are hardly aware she is there, yet she seems to know just when you are struggling to see the path ahead, and slips deftly alongside with an encouraging word to point out a track you had not noticed. The further you walk together, the more you trust her.

This is one way of imagining how Resilience might look and act if it were a person.

Writing to embody an abstract quality can help us define it more clearly and bring it alive. How you would approach this exercise? What is your picture of Resilience in human form?

The Cambridge Dictionary defines 'resilience' as 'the ability of a substance to return to its usual shape after being bent, stretched, or pressed'. And in a person, 'the ability to be happy, successful, etc., again, after something difficult or bad has happened'.

Life has no shortage of difficulties to throw at us. We are presented with repeated opportunities to exercise resilience. As Abraham Maslow wrote: 'One can choose to go back toward safety or forward toward growth. Growth must be chosen again and again; fear must be overcome again and again.'

As we practise making constructive and creative choices through whatever comes our way, what was initially difficult starts to ease. What could have brought us down has moved us on and we start to feel stronger. We have entered the re-energising process.

The resourcing process comprised an intentional moving out, to connect and equip ourselves for the journey. This sets up some momentum on our way. In the re-energising process, we keep drawing on what helps us, to strengthen and sustain this momentum. The plane has taken off and made its ascent; the task now is to keep it in the air.

We know we are in a re-energising process, as what was once alien terrain has gradually become more familiar; its challenges are less daunting, as we are more practised in meeting them. A renewed confidence and sense of purpose is strengthened by our growing wisdom, self-control, adaptability and problem-solving skills. The capacity and energy we bring to each successive situation increases.

Our energy for living beyond the limitations of loss is replenished. We have survived, and there emerges the possibility, at least, of thriving, even here. We know ourselves better — the things that have potential to trip us up, the strategies we can use to pick ourselves up again. Horizons expand, but expectations soften as an inner sense of being at home in ourselves emerges.

The re-energising process brings us into a sustainable way of living and recovering in a more rhythmic way of being. To use a running analogy, we can go all-out in a hundred metre dash, but a marathon requires us to re-adjust our pace and rhythm to match the course. We are in it for the long haul, where sustaining our energy matters more than going at speed. This also involves the wisdom to know when to deploy and where to direct that energy.

Chapter 6: Re-energising

Madeleine McCann became a household name as the little girl who went missing in the Portuguese holiday resort of Praia da Luz in May 2007, shortly before her fourth birthday. In a Radio 4 interview, her father Gerry McCann spoke of having to come to terms with how things were after approximately fifteen months into his daughter's absence. He felt he could not continue with the level of emotional intensity at which he had been living. He and his wife Kate had two other daughters who needed their care. As parents, they did not want to find their missing Madeleine any less, but they had to develop a capacity to keep going without letting all of life be claimed by grief's open wound.

Gerry McCann's shift towards embracing a re-energising process was intentional, as he recognised the realities of the onward path and what that meant for where his energies were best expended now. Re-distributing parental energy more towards the children present would cherish and strengthen the family life they had, the search for the absent child notwithstanding.

Those who have lost someone can find this particularly challenging. If we let ourselves walk on, we fear we are somehow walking out on a loved one. Only further down the road do we realise that we have not left them behind, but that they are still with us, albeit in a different way. We cannot discover this until we take the risk of moving on.

As I became willing to let go the loss of my long-desired child, I became open to forging a new way of being. I took on more writing assignments and started counselling training. Weekly trips to Leicester for a Counselling Diploma course became a way of life. I made new friends with a shared purpose, and began to look forward to our Wednesdays, learning together. My horizons broadened; I felt a new perspective emerging, and began to find some contentment. I was recovering an identity that had become somewhat buried, as well as a re-kindled momentum.

It is sometimes said that no new job proves to be as good as you had hoped, nor as bad as you had feared. I found that the reverse could also be true. My unchosen path was beginning to feel not quite as bad as I had feared, and even if it was not the good I had once hoped, there began to be periods when it was 'good enough'.

One morning in church, I watched my fellow congregation members lining up to take Communion. I was aware of so many concerns they were carrying with them: loss of a spouse; the heartache of singleness; a wayward teenager; a long-term health issue; an elderly parent slipping into dementia; job insecurity. It seemed that almost everyone had something going on — and those were only the issues I knew about. It was a reminder that the flawlessly perfect life is illusory, however much the external world promotes our entitlement to it.

At other times, I caught myself wondering whether I really even wanted this longed-for child inhabiting my imagined future. As I started to look around at parents I knew with a clearer eye, I could see that having children was not a guarantee of endless bliss, and entering into it would close other doors, of time and opportunity, currently open to me.

Further along in my journey, I interviewed a psychotherapist for an article I was writing about infertility. She spoke of her sense that everyone has been gifted with parenting energy. For some, this was expressed in biological parenting. For others, it was re-directed into other channels. Childless herself, her parenting energy was spent in a vocation of working with troubled adolescent boys. I found this concept liberating. I need not feel excluded from the parenting project; I was part of it in a different way. My unfulfilled desires did not have to be denied, but rather creatively re-directed.

In the resourcing process, we looked at connecting to the meaning that we can draw out of our difficult journeys. So significantly restorative is this that the grief expert David Kessler, co-author alongside Elisabeth Kubler-Ross on her 'five stages of loss' identified a sixth stage: 'finding meaning'. This is no glib maxim that 'everything happens for a reason'; it is about a purpose emerging from the heart of the sorrow itself, a turning to good in some form, within the actual 'stuff of life' we have found ourselves having to navigate.

I found recovering some sense of purpose in the here and now to be sustaining. I was less upended by the disappointments, insensitive remarks or other 'ouch' reminders of childlessness that had once sent me sprawling. Gaining confidence in this re-energising process helped me give myself permission not to have to attend occasions where I would struggle when feeling fragile; to have some stock responses to awkward questions mapped out, just in case. I could enjoy being 'enough' without my contentment being subject to the achievement of parenthood status.

My outlook was changing. I could not re-write my past story but I could write a new and hopeful future. Learning to lean into that approach day by day came to fruition as a re-energising process. Writing was a part of this process, too. The page had become a trusted place of consolation and support. It was a place to vent feelings safely; to identify triggers and obstacles as well as explore ways of navigating through them; to record and celebrate what had gone well or brought joy. My journal was a record-keeper, guide, friend and witness to my changing self.

Who to write

Reading through old journals can be very revealing. Recently, I reviewed one of mine from some years ago. It was as if I was reading the words of a stranger. The writer emerged as an earnest young woman, so determined to get everything right, her striving mixed with sorrow where life was not delivering her dreams. I found myself moved to compassion for the person on the page — and the aspects of her that still live within me today. In addition to the why, when, where, what and how we journal, we also have choices about *who* we are in our writing. Will we be spontaneous, or selective, in what we put down?

Social media posts are often highly selective and dressed with a positive spin. These are the gleaming shop-windows of lives that can seem so full of achievement and excitement, they leave the rest of us feeling dull or inadequate by comparison. But if you ever have a face-to-face catch-up with a friend with whom you connect primarily on Facebook, you will soon discover what is really going on behind the scenes.

Writing in a journal for our eyes only enables us to write spontaneously, free of concerns about how our words might impact others. Yet even here, we may find ourselves being unconsciously selective.

I once led a group free-writing exercise where one participant was astonished as she read back over her words to find she had written about everyone else except herself. She realised that her non-appearance on the page reflected how she interacted with others in life generally. How is your writing balanced? What are its preoccupations or omissions? It can be as telling to see what we do not write about as what we *do*.

Who is the self we are putting on the page? To be fruitful, a journal needs to be a place where we can be open, truthful and real. Earlier in this book, a writing exercise suggested completing sentences that contain the word 'really'; for example, 'What I really want/think/need.' Working with these can help us start digging down beneath our stock answers and assumptions to what might be going on underneath.

A journal can also help us face the challenges of living authentically. As we read what we have written, we can ask ourselves to what extent who we are on the page aligns with who we are being out in the world. Any mismatches and anomalies can be useful areas to explore.

As human beings, we experience a wide range of moods and emotions. We may pick up the pen in different emotional states. Who we are in our writing may be our sad, angry, hopeful or anxious self. As you read your journal, do particular emotions stand out? Are you more likely to write as your excited self or your depressed self? Or perhaps it is your more dispassionate, reflective self that is given a voice.

We are also complex creatures. Different parts of us live within, as sub-personalities. These inner, active elements have developed in response to different rewards, punishments and experiences at various stages of our lives.

Is there a particular part of you journalling today? Could it be the voice of a sub-personality wanting some special attention? A rebel or a people-pleaser? A 'spoiled brat' or 'inner disciplinarian'? Perfectionist, critic, victim or Worry Warrior? Or something else?

It helps to take time to discern and name our sub-personalities, as we recognise their various voices. They are not trouble-makers to be quashed. Worked with creatively, our sub-personalities have something to contribute to our growth and well-being as we seek to integrate them into our whole self. Journalling can help us to engage with them.

Once we have identified the voice of a particular sub-personality, we can dialogue with it on the page, or even create a dialogue between two sub-personalities whose voices are in conflict. By giving each part a hearing, we can resolve inner collisions and draw the best out of each one.

There is also the 'who' we want to become. A journal can be a sanctuary to explore the quieter, shyer voices in us that need nurturing. Perhaps we want to foster a more assertive self, rehearsing on paper something we want to speak out in a real-life situation. Or strengthen a currently fragile presence of joy or hope. For example, how would it be to write as a grateful or peaceful person? What would we notice?

We can take on the spirit of playfulness and experiment by writing from a less familiar — and perhaps less comfortable — way of being, seeing what might shift in the process. Our writing may be transformative, suggesting ways we can turn what we explore on the page into a blueprint for action out in the world.

Journalling also enables us to reconnect with or release who we have been in the past. Writing a compassionate letter to our past self, or an encouraging letter from our self at some point in the future, may help us free our potential in the present. The journal can become a time-machine, helping us meet and integrate who we have been and who we might become.

There are times when we feel we have lost ourselves and the sense of our own identity. This can happen particularly in seasons of difficulty and upheaval. In this state, it is enough to write simply *as we are*, without having to define *who we are*. Our words may seem thrown down like random pebbles on the ground, but as we persevere, we may find that in reading them back later, we see shapes and patterns we were blind to at the time. Our journal becomes our mirror, revealing who we are, and sustaining us along the way.

Phil's Story: Writing as Sustenance

Phil has used writing as a resource through various challenging journeys over the years. 'I'd advise anyone wondering whether writing could help them through difficult times simply to try it for themselves,' he says.

He has written in different ways at different times. Over thirty years ago, when going through a period of Jungian analysis, Phil wrote about his sessions and the dreams he was having. Later, he used the List technique, writing a list of resentments as he progressed through the forth step of the recovery process with Alcoholics Anonymous. Phil says, 'Even though it was just a list, the process of writing had quite an impact on me.'

In 2016, Phil underwent chemotherapy treatment for Lymphoma, after an initial diagnosis at a very early stage in 2011. He kept a diary for most of the six months that he underwent treatment. Although he has rarely read back over it since, as he finds it 'rather frightening to think about that period', Phil says that the writing process helped him along the way:

'At the time, it felt important to have somewhere to write about how scared I was feeling and the different things that happened as I went through it. It felt as if I was doing something that was in some way permanent.'

Writing about difficult times can not only enable us to find words for our feelings, but also help us to clarify and give shape to our own story.

Phil later wrote the narrative of his experience of illness for others to read — specifically a Lymphoma Group on Facebook. Below is part of that piece, followed by an extract of personal writing with a more reflective slant, from Phil's *Chemo Diary*.

'I was diagnosed in 2011 aged 50, following a biopsy on a pea-sized lump at the top of my thigh. The initial diagnosis left me shocked and confused. Initially, I was graded as Stage 1 and put onto "watch and wait". Over time, my lymphoma grew and spread. More lumps appeared at the top of my thigh, then my right arm pit. Scans revealed several sizeable masses in my abdomen, one of which doubled in size in less than a year. Words fail me when I try to express the horror and stress of that life, with lumps slowly appearing and expanding throughout my body.

'In July 2016, at a routine clinic visit the haematologist saw my blood results on the screen, turned to me and said, "I think it's time to start treatment." I just kind of nodded; she had spoken so gently and calmly that it reminded me of the way my Mum used to tell my Dad that the dog needed to be taken out for a walk. Minutes later I heard her telling the medical secretaries to rearrange appointments, saying: "He's Stage 4, he needs to start now!"

'After three cycles of treatment the haematologist told me that it wasn't working very well; only 20% tumour shrinkage when they usually expect at least 50%. That was my lowest point: desolation, panic and despair. However, my red cell levels were going up, my spleen was returning to normal size and I didn't want to give up so easily. There aren't that many treatment options. So, we agreed to try two more cycles and it suddenly started to work, giving 70 to 80% shrinkage. By the end, all the lumps and tumours which had riddled my body had melted away. Miraculous.

Chapter 6: Re-energising

Tuesday 22nd November 2016

'Another night without night sweats. Went to The Countess Hospital to see Dr B and she ushered me into her office with the words, "fantastic scan results, really good shrinkage".

'She went on to tell me that above the diaphragm, there is nothing really above 1cm, that my spleen has gone back to 9cm from 16cm and that below the diaphragm, my tumours have shrunk by 70 to 80%, which counts as a good partial response. I was so happy that I cried a bit.

'I wonder what did the trick? Was it the additional exercise that I have been doing to try and counteract the muscle-wasting effects of the Prednisolone, or was it the visualisations, or was it eating meat, or was it just that my body needed more time? I don't know. I walked out of there feeling like I was floating on air, like a huge weight had been lifted from me.'

In the Re-energising process, writing may help you to:

- Maintain internal order and priorities
- Track patterns and respond swiftly
- Plan challenges not taken on before
- Think outside the box
- Embrace life in all its facets
- Regain equilibrium
- Stay focussed on new goals
- Savour presence, not productivity

Journalling Suggestions

> Maintain internal order and priorities

Headspace Audit

Take a page in your journal, or a separate blank sheet that you can attach later. In the centre, write down **My Mind**, and from that central point, map out what your mind is focussing on at the moment — the things that occupy your attention (family, work, home, activities, achievements, concerns, etc.)

Map these out from your 'mind-centre', using lines, circles or other shapes of appropriate sizes. Write words inside these to indicate what is filling your headspace. Take time to tune in to your thoughts, using your intuition and creativity to chart their significance and how they relate to one another. Come back to the centre each time, when you start a new thought.

Afterwards, look over what you have created.

- What do you notice?
- Is there a dominant theme or aspect taking over your headspace?
- Is there anything significant that is being squeezed out?
- What puzzles, interests or surprises you?

Now you can see what your mind is up to, are there adjustments you want to make, new habits to train or actions to undertake? (For example, I wanted to adjust my mind's preoccupation with future to become more attentive to the present.)

Take five minutes to write about your reflections and conclusions. This exercise can be repeated at any time. It can be enlightening to compare how what occupies your headspace changes — or not.

> Track patterns and respond swiftly

Identifying Buttons

Think back over your recent past and identify three incidents that:

 * involved another person
 * left you feeling troubled or upset in some way.

These do not have to be very dramatic or traumatic; they may just be part of the ups and downs of daily living. If you can, take them from different areas of your life, i.e. work, home and social circle.

Spend a few minutes writing about each of these incidents in more detail. As you describe them, pay attention to exactly what it was that you found upsetting. Describe how you felt, as you seek to pinpoint the heart of the matter. For example, if someone took your lunch from the work fridge, what emotion did that trigger in you? Anger at the unfairness or disrespect? Frustration at inconvenience, a sense of loss, feeling powerless or simply hungry?

Re-read your three pieces and see if you can notice any connections. Do these incidents suggest an underlying raw nerve or vulnerability? If the common thread of a particular button being pushed becomes evident, reflect on whether you can recall how far this sort of feeling goes back. Does it originate in a situation or incident from a long time past? Some significant buttons can be installed in childhood.

Write a few sentences about what you have discerned. If you have identified a well-worn pattern that belongs to an earlier time, is this something that you want to update and adjust? What fresh choices would you like to make about how you respond to what happens in the here and now? How can you separate old reactions from new situations? What practical steps could you take to manage the feelings they may set off in you?

> Plan challenges not taken on before

Writing the 4 *R*'s

As we become more settled, we may find ourselves more open to embracing new challenges. One way of exploring these and charting a way forward is to structure some writing under four headings:

Reach, Rewards, Resources & Roadblocks

Divide your page into four sections and head each with one of the R's above. Next, write some notes and reflections under each heading.

Reach: Identify what it is you aim to do or achieve. What is the 'reach' of this goal? If it is too easy you will lose interest; too far beyond your grasp and you may give up. You may need to break down an ambitious reach into smaller steps.

Rewards: What are you hoping for from this venture? Are its rewards emotional/mental? Relational? Physical or spiritual? Financial or material? How much do you really want these benefits? Clarify what motivates you.

Resources: What resources will enable you, and how will you access them? Identify your own inner qualities alongside the outside help you need —

information, other people in your personal or professional support network, time, money.

Roadblocks: What might be the obstacles along the way? Can you anticipate any difficulties within and without (especially if this is something you have tried before)? How will you deal with these things? It helps to be prepared.

As you re-read what you have written, note down what you most need at this point and identify steps you need to take towards your goal. What is the one thing you can do right now, as a first step on your way?

> Think outside the box

Resilience Miracle

Consider these five skills of resilience:

- Emotional regulation: the ability to be emotionally self-aware, and express and manage emotions without becoming overwhelmed.
- Optimistic mind-set: the ability to see the possibilities and opportunities in challenging issues, despite the difficulties.
- Problem-solving: the ability to find and act on creative, new solutions when a problem is identified.
- Supportive connection: the ability to grow a social network of healthy relationships and to reach out for help when needed.
- Self-care: the ability to prioritise looking after personal well-being of body, mind and spirit, to be equipped for whatever life brings.

Choose the one of these skills that you sense most needs strengthening in yourself.

Imagine that overnight, the 'Resilience Fairy' passes by and tips a bucketful of this quality over you as you sleep.

As you wake the next morning, how are you different? What do you do that indicates a new abundance of this quality in you? What might others notice about how you are living? Use your imagination to free-write your response to this. Be as specific as you can, e.g.:

- What emotion are you aware of and what fresh choices do you make in managing it?

- What previously missed opportunities are you seeing in an issue you have?
- What creative new solutions are emerging from an old problem?
- Where and with whom are you fostering connections?
- How are you looking after yourself more intentionally?

As you write about these things, what suggests itself to you as something you could actually put into practice today, to develop this skill of resilience?

Poetry Exploration

> Embrace life in all its facets

A Northern Morning

It rained from dawn. The fire died in the night.
I poured hot water on some foreign leaves;
I brought the fire to life. Comfort
spread from the kitchen like a taste of chocolate
through the head-waters of a body,
accompanied by that little-water-music.
The knotted veins of the old house tremble and carry
a louder burden: the audience joining in.

People are peaceful in a world so lavish
with the ingredients of life:
the world of breakfast easy as Tahiti.
But we must leave. Head down in my new coat
I dodge to the High Street conscious of my fellows
damp and sad in their vegetable fibres.
But by the bus-stop I look up: the spring trees
exult in the downpour, radiant, clean for hours:
This is the life! This is the only life!

Alistair Elliot

This poem embraces the realities of a Northern morning. But the rainy, cold light of dawn is not met with despondency; the poem's Speaker is active, generating comfort by rekindling the fire and making tea before heading out into the wet streets.

Throughout the poem, water is transformed from dampener to life-giver, becoming the little-water-music that runs throughout. Hot water makes the tea. The rain's downpour washes the trees, a cleansing of the natural world that uplifts the Speaker and ends the poem on a note of joy. Who would wish to be anywhere else but here, tasting life in all the fullness of an ordinary Northern morning?

It is easy to take things for granted, yet there is much to savour in the simple pleasures of our surroundings and everyday rituals. Take an ordinary morning in your household and write about what makes it 'lavish/ with the ingredients of life'. You could list these as ingredients in the recipe of your day. You may wish to linger over each one by adding a sentence or two celebrating what you most appreciate about it.

The poem's Speaker is undaunted by the morning's inconveniences and frustrations. They simply set right what they can or adapt to meet the day's conditions as they are. In doing so, joy breaks through.

Can you think of an occasion when you met some challenging circumstances with resilience and creativity? Perhaps you faced some hitches or glitches in a planned event or journey? Such times often become the stories we later tell with a smile.

Starting with 'It was a time when…', write about a situation when you engaged with some less than perfect conditions and found your way through. Conclude with a few sentences reflecting on what feels important as you write about this.

> Regain equilibrium

This Morning

I watched the sun moving round the kitchen,
an early spring sun that strengthened and weakened,
coming and going like an old mind.

I watched like one bedridden for a long time
on their first journey back into the world
who finds it enough to be going on with:

the way the sunlight brought each possession in turn
to its attention and made of it a small still life:

the iron frying pan gleaming on its hook like an ancient find,
the powdery green cheek of a bruised clementine.

Though more beautiful still was how the light moved on,
letting go each chair and coffee cup without regret

the way my grandmother, in her final year, received me:
neither surprised by my presence, nor distressed by my leaving,
content, though, while I was there.

Esther Morgan

This poem's precision of image and elegant, unhurried tone gives it the quality of a 'small still life'. There is a quiet beauty in how it takes time to observe the precise effect of the morning sun's light moving across the kitchen. The Speaker tracks the light's measured pace, becoming drawn into its patient attention. What moments can you take today to watch and align with some aspect of the natural world?

Notice how it is only in the last three lines that the poem turns from the progress of the slow-moving sunlight to address an aspect of the Speaker's own life directly. Image and experience are interwoven, to bring a sense of peace at the poem's conclusion.

One way of writing with a poem is to adopt its form as a template to contain and shape your own material. Choose something to observe — something living in the world around you that holds a particular resonance. It might be a plant or a creature, an aspect of the landscape — or something completely different that catches your attention. Follow the poem's outline and complete it with your own words, so you have:

- Title (which you may fill in afterwards)
- I watched… (three descriptive lines)
- I watched… (three more descriptive lines)

- the way… (two lines on something you notice about what you see)
- (Two lines with more detail related to what you notice)
- Though more _____ still was (fill in the blank with your own adjective, and continue for two lines)
- the way… (three lines linking some aspect of what you have described to an aspect of your own life — a situation, something or someone).

How did you find this exercise of stepping into the poem's structure?

> Stay focussed on new goals

The Art of Disappearing

When they say Don't I know you?
say no.

When they invite you to the party
remember what parties are like

before answering.
Someone is telling you in a loud voice
they once wrote a poem.
Greasy sausage balls on a paper plate.

Then reply.

If they say We should get together
say why?

It's not that you don't love them anymore.
You're trying to remember something
too important to forget.
Trees. The monastery bell at twilight.
Tell them you have a new project.
It will never be finished.

When someone recognizes you in a grocery store
nod briefly and become a cabbage.
When someone you haven't seen in ten years
appears at the door,

don't start singing him all your new songs.
You will never catch up.

Walk around feeling like a leaf.
Know you could tumble any second.
Then decide what to do with your time.

Naomi Shihab Nye

Resilience implies a growing capacity to know what is important to you and to sustain a focus on your deeper priorities, irrespective of the distractions and obstacles that threaten to knock them off-centre. Often, it is not the big issues that get in the way, but an accumulation of small things. A friend described this to me as like 'being nibbled to death by ducks'.

How do you respond to the strategies the Speaker suggests the Reader employs when interrupted by these unwanted situations? Do they relate to your own experience? Are there any you would add?

Put your own distractions into this form, by writing them from lines beginning,

'When they…', and/or 'If they…' And follow this with the advice you would give to yourself in such circumstances.

> Savour presence, not productivity

Camas Lilies

Consider the lilies of the field,
the blue banks of camas opening
into acres of sky along the road.
Would the longing to lie down
and be washed by that beauty
abate if you knew their usefulness,
how the natives ground their bulbs
for flour, how the settlers' hogs
uprooted them, grunting in gleeful
oblivion as the flowers fell?
And you—what of your rushed

and useful life? Imagine setting it all down—
papers, plans, appointments, everything—
leaving only a note: "Gone
to the fields to be lovely. Be back
when I'm through with blooming."
Even now, unneeded and uneaten,
the camas lilies gaze out above the grass
from their tender blue eyes.
Even in sleep your life will shine.
Make no mistake. Of course
your work will always matter.
Yet Solomon in all his glory
was not arrayed like one of these.

Lynn Ungar

This poem reminds us that there are times to turn away from our relentless urge to be productive and simply cherish the beauty of presence.

Its opening echoes part of the Bible's Sermon on the Mount, where Jesus calls his listeners' attention to 'the lilies of the field'. In the poem, the Speaker considers the blue camas lilies, and is captivated by their beauty, irrespective of their usefulness as a source of food. We are encouraged to identify with these lilies. As they hold our gaze, they silently remind us of the unconscious beauty that shines through whatever lives and grows.

Give yourself permission to step away from your daily tasks to seek beauty rather than pursue usefulness. You could take a walk round your garden, neighbourhood, park or even zoo. Take time with an animal or some natural plant, tree, flower, object or place. Set aside any thoughts of use or function and seek to see what you are looking at for itself.

Write about the qualities that catch your attention. What is the most striking feature of this natural being, the one you would most like to be in tune with?

In the poem, the Speaker asks us to imagine leaving an absence note to cover our departure from our daily routine. What note would you like to leave and where? Where would you like to go and what would you like to do? Could you leave a note and do just that?

Chapter 6: Re-energising

How would you answer the Speaker's questions in lines 4-12? Does seeing the usefulness of something obscure your engagement with its beauty? Think about objects you use everyday. Is there a beauty about some of these that you are missing?

Write about an aspect of beauty in something ordinary — for example, a toothbrush, kitchen item or piece of furniture.

When you find yourself…	Writing may help you to…
• Grounded in a new rhythm	• Maintain internal order and priorities
• Knowing how to engage the territory	• Track patterns and respond swiftly
• Open to a new destination	• Plan challenges not taken on before
• Having greater capacity to adapt	• Think outside the box
• Recovering hope	• Embrace life in all its facets
• More able to overcome knock-backs	• Regain equilibrium
• With a re-located sense of purpose	• Stay focussed on new goals
• In a sustainable way of being	• Savour presence, not productivity

Chapter 7: Resolving

- Seeing clearly the way one has come
- Drawing a line, even if short of ideal
- Facing the reality of a goal met
- Sensing an endpoint in self/situation
- At peace in a new configuration
- Discerning the start of a new season
- Feeling relieved and more settled
- Reaching or releasing your goal

Where did I see it? Online? In a magazine? Wherever, I had been reading about *More to Life*, an organisation supporting those who find themselves involuntarily infertile and are looking to chart a new, meaningful course beyond their own unwanted journey.

The charity was promoting a memorial service at one of the London Hospitals. At this, participants were invited to mark the end of their striving to become biological parents; to mourn their loss and move towards hope for a different future.

The concept struck me powerfully. Those who have not experienced infertility's pain can find it hard to understand its connection to the sense of bereavement. 'No-one has lived', they say, and so, 'no-one has died.' But the child you desire has lived in your head and heart for a long, long time; a real person who inhabits the landscape of your assumed future. This is the child who needs to be relinquished, but turning off the life-support machine of a cherished hope is not easy to do.

When I saw the *More to Life* material, I wanted to write an article about the memorial service for the Church Times. My proposal was accepted and I wrote the piece, drawing on and including my own experience, with photographs to boot. After it was published, I reflected that much about my personal journey of infertility was now out in print, and I was not distressed by it. Once, it had felt raw and intrusive to expose my deep, unanswered longings to the world; now, it was far less of a deal. Perhaps, I thought, I am really coming to terms with what has been such a painful issue. A new sense of ease had crept up on me slowly.

The process of re-energising and simply staying on the road had slipped into a process of resolving. There was a sense of peace at this quiet shutting of doors that I had never anticipated. Something had fallen into place.

As we travel along unwanted paths, we accumulate consolations and support, sometimes from unexpected places. We discover ways of living with our original dreams unfulfilled, which can lead to a contentment to walk on without aiming or aching for the endpoint. Paradoxically, as we *live* more in the process, the resolution of our journey finds its own way to meet us.

Processes can shift almost unconsciously, rather as in recovery of an illness when we suddenly realise, for example, that we are not coughing so much, or we can put weight on a foot in a way we could not the previous day. It is not that we conspire to reach a new place, more that we consent to let go of the old one. Sometimes this letting go feels intentional, at others it is an easing that happens whilst our attention is engaged elsewhere.

It takes hindsight to see what has been going on as our journeys of loss unfold in their own, unique rhythm. Although it can be hard to define, there does come a time when we sense our journey is coming to its final chapters, that some sort of watershed has been reached, even if the destination is different from what we once imagined. And even if the resolving is in the delightful coming to pass of the original dream, its reality will feel different. The journey will have changed us.

I have been told many stories of those who gave up on having children, only to find themselves expecting a baby just as they were willing to live child-free. But this is not a foolproof formula. We cannot give up what we long for as a strategy for making it happen. Believe me, we tried! All we can do is open the door to possibilities and foster a willingness to accept whatever emerges. We release our hope to embrace a wider picture, reflecting the insights of the medieval mystic Julian of Norwich's visions during her illness, that: 'All shall be well, and all shall be well and all manner of things shall be well.'

Whether it emerges as a growing awareness, an insight arising from hindsight or in the fulfilling of our earlier desire, the resolving process is more than a line crossed. It is a sense of coming to live in a new place, with an acceptance of how things have worked out for us, free of resentment or regret.

It can take a while to settle into our way of being in this territory. Someone who had come through significant health issues with both cancer and arthritis told me: 'People keep asking me what is the new normal. I really struggle with this. I don't feel normal at all.'

'And what happens,' said another, 'if there is no resolution? What if you are living with an unwanted state of affairs forever?'

Resolving is not merely an external issue. There can be an internal resolving of a situation that is ongoing, but which we come to walk with in a new way. One creative aspect of the resolving process is learning to live with the loose ends and unanswered questions that refuse to shift or be tidied away. In this process, we allow ourselves to feel at home in their company as a permanent, rather than provisional, state of affairs.

These days, my involuntary infertility feels like an old war wound: it does not trouble me most of the time. Occasionally, I may wince as a sore point gets pressed — a Mothering Sunday Service, perhaps, or an enthusiastic friend talking about their children or grandchildren. I wonder, and can worry, about who will be my advocate in old age. But rather than be cast down, I use these glitches as opportunities for creative choices. I can acknowledge the stings honestly, letting the feelings *be* there. I can choose to exercise kindness in these circumstances: perhaps to allow myself to rejoice with my friends; to make time to enjoy an activity I could not do if I were looking after children; and to trust to the future, whilst remaining connected to the wider family community to which I belong now. Occasional tears are part of the territory, but I can echo the poet of the Psalms who declares that: 'The boundary lines have fallen for me in good places.'[1]

American psychologist Pauline Boss has coined the term 'ambiguous loss' to reflect her study of those whose losses have left them with particular loose ends: relatives of dementia sufferers; of soldiers gone missing in action; of victims of 9/11. She notes how our Western mindset tends to approach grieving as a set of tasks to be worked through, with boxes ticked at each stage. Yet, the resolving of grief can be in accepting those elements

---

[1] The Bible, Psalm 16:6

of it that remain. Our grief is no longer dominant, but it has not disappeared; it has been integrated into the life we have re-grown around, and beyond, it. Accepting this 'incompleteness' brings relief. It takes the pressure off having to achieve permanent happiness, and gives permission for sorrow to rise as it needs to.

The resolving process is multi-layered and can come upon us like waves of an incoming tide. For example, the physical resolving of a major health issue is just one part of recovery. Being discharged from treatment may signal the start of some emotional, psychological or spiritual aspects of our journey, as we process what has happened, what it means for life now, and how it impacts our way of living, relationships and personal priorities.

As we continue to use writing as a personal resource, we are building a record of our journey to look back on. Re-reading some of our journal entries at a much later date can also support us as we realise how much has been changing along the way. Sometimes, people are astonished at the differences between how they feel now compared to how they felt then. It brings an assurance that hard terrain can soften, intractable situations resolve. We can come to a new place.

We may find, too, that we become more confident in sharing our writing, and discover that we do not journey alone.

Writing with and for others

Throughout this book, I have emphasised the primacy of privacy in journalling. You can enjoy the freedom of writing with no holds barred when you know you are the only one who will read it. You can be completely honest, with neither fear of others' judgement, nor the compulsion to justify yourself. You can work through things as they truly are, trusting the page as a reliable and non-intrusive listener.

If you feel isolated writing on your own, you may choose to write alongside others in a library, or by joining a silent Zoom writing session online. Writing here remains private, company notwithstanding. Committing to such writing settings can help you hold yourself to account in maintaining your journalling practice, as well as minimising distraction. Your writing belongs to you, but you can, of course, choose to share it with someone you trust will hear you with empathy and respect. It may be a friend, counsellor or other confidante you are inviting into your inner world, as you disclose some thing precious or seek help in exploring some thing important.

Joining a journal-writing group goes one stage further: in this dedicated space, you not only commit to writing alongside others, you may also share some of your writing with the group. A journalling group is a place to explore fresh approaches, with the leader's choice of writing prompts inevitably different from what you might pick for yourself.

One of my own group members, Ruth, says: 'Each time I attend, I come away with new ideas for journalling. It's revitalising my writing and uplifting my mood.' She feels that a journalling group 'gives vital encouragement and challenge through live connection and presence', providing 'a safe space where we feel held, able to be authentic and respect one another'. Another, Diane, enjoys 'the sense of having my voice heard in an otherwise noisy world'.

Listening to others can be valuable, too. Pauline appreciates 'hearing others' musings which can then push your writing to a different level or in a different direction.' And if you do feel diffident about disclosing your content, you can still share your experience of the process of a writing exercise.

It is vital to be aware of the sort of group where you share personal writing. I have been part of a poetry workshop where a participant presented a poem about selling her house after a divorce, only for a couple of workshop members to launch into a merciless critique. She was left deeply hurt and never shared her writing there again.

Part of the problem was the nature of the group. It was, after all, a writing workshop, so participants felt free to respond to the writing purely on its literary qualities. A workshop with a therapeutic purpose would have been a better choice for a more considerate response to what the words meant to the poet. She had also offered this personal poem at a stage when its issues were still very raw. When sharing your writing, you need to reflect on how much you have emotionally invested in it. It may just be a matter of timing. If you expose deeply personal material too widely, too early, another's cool critique can feel devastating. Better to wait until you are able to be a little more objective and are less emotionally vulnerable.

You may be considering publishing your words online or in print. In recent years, there has been a growing trend to share journeys through difficult times with a wider public. It is something to consider carefully. Publishing our writing takes things to another level.

When I write for myself, my writing remains in my domain. Even if I disclose some of it to those I trust, I can moderate and interpret my words for my chosen listener or reader. When it comes to publication, my writing 'leaves home' to make its own way in the world. It will be read by those I may never meet, and needs to connect with others on its own merits. Considerations such as accuracy of spelling, grammar and clarity of style come into play when communicating to a wider readership. The writing itself becomes subject to others' response and critique, with diverse opinions — right or wrong — about both quality and content.

So, consider why you want to go public. You may wish to offer your experience to help or inform your reader, or highlight an issue you feel needs addressing. It is not uncommon for people to find themselves writing the book they wish they had been able to read when they were struggling with their particular challenges, but if the aim of publication is to validate your writing, take care not to confuse this with being about validating *you*. And as for making your fortune…

Think, too, about how far you are along the line in processing your material. If your issues stir overwhelming emotions in you, go gently in what and where you share. You do not have to have resolved everything before going public, but you do need to have reached a level of detachment, and capacity for objectivity. Others' comments on your writing may lack empathy or understanding; it is never easy to hear negative criticism, so do not make it more difficult than it need be.

It is also the case that things change — both in our situations and ourselves. The most valuable words about getting through tough times tend to be from those who have made it through the storm, rather than those in the midst. Waiting a little before putting it all out there may enhance your material with a wider perspective and deeper insight.

When I wrote my piece for the Church Times, I was not unduly troubled by disclosing parts of my personal story. The disclosure was part of the resolution and, I later realised, an expression of it.

Sharing the experience of our unwanted journeys can be powerful. It can encourage others, validate the experience of those going through something similar and give a voice to something that needs to be heard.

But there are questions to think about. Why might you want to tell the world your story? What is the return you are looking for? How much hangs on this?

Linda's Story: Writing for Yourself First

In 1982, 18-year-old Linda arrived in South Africa as a reluctant immigrant; her mother had insisted she should not split the family by staying behind. They lived in a small, predominantly Afrikaans town during and after Apartheid. Linda hated it. She describes the tense run-up to 'the first free and fair election', in 1994:

'People (including us) stockpiled food, candles, water, petrol, weapons, ammunition. I had a small bag packed with my most precious belongings. I was ready to go at a moment's notice. My husband often worked away and I was in a state of permanent distress. I had the TV on all day in case civil war broke out. After the election, fear of civil war dissipated but the violence grew as people realised that life would not immediately and dramatically improve. Many became angry and decided to take what they felt was their due. People we knew or knew of were attacked and killed at home, in their cars, and elsewhere.'

Linda left South Africa in 1996: 'I practically ran out of the country, and cried only for the dog we had to leave behind.'

Looking back, Linda senses she went through Post-Traumatic Stress over the ensuing years. She has always written, so naturally turned to words to process her experience. She wrote at home, intermittently, for approximately twenty years, initially writing poetry about her personal experiences and emotions, as well as about others' experiences. As the number of poems grew, she started a blog, posting roughly a poem a day. Realising that many of them needed putting into context, she added explanations of the prompts and thinking behind each poem. She found writing both poetry and accompanying prose cathartic: 'Whenever I obsessed about something that had occurred, about how I felt and was affected, I let a little more of the trauma go. The blog posts accompanying each poem were the best thing I ever did to excise my demons. As I explained myself to my readers, I began to understand myself.'

Once every poem and its story were shared, Linda shut down her blog. 'I felt – for want of a better word – cured: writing over a long period of time, and time itself, of course, allowed me to heal. Sharing my story with others was massively helpful: I was honest about what happened, about how it made me feel, about the part I played living under an oppressive regime. There's a huge sense of relief when you are honest with the world and with yourself.'

Linda stresses the importance of honesty for anyone writing through tough times. 'Whether you are a victim or complicit in something you regret, lying to yourself kills you a little each day.'

This makes privacy paramount: 'Writing about your trauma certainly helps, but you must do it for yourself and not worry about anything you write being seen by others. If you later choose to share your writing, that's great; but do it for yourself first.'

Autumn of 2024 saw the publication of *Tales from the Rainbow Nation*, Linda's poetry and prose memoir of her time in South Africa, but her poems from that period have been making an impact for much longer. *The View From In Here*, about censorship, has travelled far and wide. Since being anthologised by the Human Rights Commission and the University of London, in association with Keats House Poets, it has been published in an e-zine; read at a memorial service for Nelson Mandela; translated into Italian for a website review; used by an A-Level Art student; referenced by a teacher on Facebook; and led to a young journalist living in India, who had read the anthology, contacting her for an interview.

'What makes me laugh is that I'm not sure it even is a poem, as it is mostly redacted words and blank space. I wrote it for myself but it has affected a number of people in different ways: writing can do that.'

This, and another of Linda's poems, are below:

The View From In Here

Afrikaners share their declared birthright,
thus Uitlanders don't feel contrite.
Migrants ignore what they should deplore:

Apartheid's all right if you're white.

(Uitlander: foreigner)

Pre-Election Jitters

Civil war is on the tip of the country's tongue.
You might have to flee for your life:
what do you pack in your truck?

Dried goods
Canned food
Water
Candles
Matches
Can opener
Two 25 gallon drums of petrol
Ammunition for the firearm you keep at your hip
A map to Zimbabwe

The things you need to survive.

You fear the day is coming soon.
You might be one of the lucky few
to be airlifted out of the country
by your former government.
What do you pack in your tiny suitcase?

Family photographs
Video tapes of your baby
His first curl
The battered jewellery box
that was a gift from your parents
on your 11th birthday
The jewellery in it
(inexpensive; sentimental)

The things you need to survive
to make surviving matter.

In the Resolving process, writing may help you to:

- Clarify key marker points
- Note differences between then and now
- Explore experience versus expectation
- Explore indications of ending
- Ground this new way of being
- Clarify what is emerging
- Celebrate calmer waters
- Find a way of marking the spot

Journalling Suggestions

> Clarify key marker points

How Did I Get Here?

In the process of 'resolving', you are better placed to reflect on what has gone before and has brought you to this point. Hindsight enables you to pinpoint more accurately the shifts along your journey's path. When I have counselled those recovering from burn-out, we have reflected on how far back the build-up of pressure began. Identifying the early signs of things going awry can help us notice and respond earlier, to avoid repeating a previous crisis.

Ira Progoff, creator of a comprehensive journalling programme for personal development, includes an activity he calls 'Stepping Stones'. This technique tracks one's life through key points of transition.

Imagine your progress through life as crossing a river. The idea is to identify the stepping stones that have formed the stages along your way. Progoff suggests starting with a first stone of 'I am born' and progressing to the present day. You are encouraged not to exceed twelve stages. You write these down as heading, then you put them into chronological order and choose one or two to free-write about in more detail, starting with 'It was a time when.'

Progoff's approach can be adapted to track your particular unwanted journey; take a few moments to note down significant signs and symptoms along its trajectory. You are looking to answer the question: 'how did I get here?'

You may find yourself most aware of factors in the recent past, when the signs had become more insistent. So, as you track back, keep asking yourself whether you can discern anything earlier. How far back can you go?

Now write about one or two stages in more detail: explore how things were, outside and within you, and what actions you took – or did not take – in response.

Suspend self-judgement as much as you can. Put yourself back in your shoes as you were then, to gain an understanding of what factors were at play in the choices you made.

> Note differences between then and now

Postcards to the Past

Imagine yourself at the top of a mountain trail. As you stand at the summit,

- What does it feel like?
- What can you see around you?
- Does it look how you imagined?

Looking back down the slope, you see different figures at various points on the mountain trail you have just ascended. You are able to write some notes to them, which can be placed along the pathway for the climbers to find.

What words of guidance, encouragement and wisdom do you want to communicate to those still on the ascent? What would have helped your past, climbing self to hear from your present self at the summit? Write a few postcard-length messages for those on the trail below and decide where you want to place each one.

> Explore experience vs. expectation

Hopes and Fears Reality Check

Our plans and expectations for the future are rarely an exact fit for the reality that arrives.

Yet these mismatches between what we anticipate and what we meet can be fruitful places that help us grow, drawing out qualities of acceptance and adaptability, courage and creativity, gratitude and joy.

Write your response to the following prompts, working through them twice. Firstly, take a situation where your hopes were dashed. Secondly, take a situation where your fears proved groundless. These may be situations you chose or ones chosen for you.

* What were your expectations about this event/situation (and what led you to make these assumptions)?
* How did the reality differ from what you anticipated (and what factors — positive or negative — had not been on your radar at all)?
* How did you respond (from feelings to coping strategies)?
* Looking back, is there anything you could, or would, have done differently (without adding a '*should*')?
* What did you learn from that time, that you can take forward?

Summarise your overall reflections in a few sentences. Do you think you have learnt more from disappointed expectations or groundless fears, or were they just different things? How might this impact your outlook about future events and plans?

> Explore indications of ending

Proprioceptive Writing

'But little by little…
….there was a new voice
which you slowly
recognised as your own'

So writes the poet Mary Oliver in her poem *The Journey*. Perhaps you have been gradually reconnecting with your own voice as you have journalled and navigated your own unique journey.

One way to foster this inner listening is the Proprioceptive Writing technique. This was devised in the 1970's by Linda Trichter Metcalf to help students find their writing voice. Its title is derived from the Latin '*proprius*', which means 'one's own.' The approach interweaves free-writing, with reflection en route.

By incorporating reflection alongside expression in this way, the proprioceptive technique encourages a healthy balance between the two. Its measured pace fosters a deeper inner listening and the making of insightful connections.

To practise, find a quiet and hospitable space to write for approximately 25 minutes. Lighting a candle and playing some Baroque music are also suggested as ways of setting a calm atmosphere for this writing. Bring your attention to an area you wish to explore. For this exercise, you could focus on how aspects of your life come to fruition, a resolving, or a moving on in some way.

Seek to listen to what comes to mind, and write what you hear. As you write, be aware of what is going down on the page. When something catches your particular attention, ask yourself the key proprioceptive question: 'What do I mean by this?' As your answer comes to mind, write that down, perhaps by starting a new sentence with, 'What I mean by this is....' as you continue writing.

After you have finished this slow dance between free-writing and reflection, re-read your writing, perhaps out loud, so you literally voice your thoughts. Tell your story with curiosity, not judgement.

Ask yourself how you feel now, and what thoughts were heard but not written down. Does this writing suggest any further proprioceptive writing you may wish to do?

Poetry Exploration

> Explore indications of ending

The Way It Is

Over and over we break
open, we break and
we break and we open.
For a while, we try to fix
the vessel—as if
to be broken is bad.
As if with glue and tape
and a steady hand we
might bring things to perfect
again. As if they were ever
perfect. As if to be broken is not
also perfect. As if to be open
is not the path toward joy.

The vase that's been shattered
and cracked will never
hold water. Eventually
it will leak. And at some
point, perhaps, we decide
that we're done with picking
our flowers anyway, and no
longer need a place to contain them
We watch them grow just
as wildflowers do—unfenced,
unmanaged, blossoming only
when they're ready—and mygod,
how beautiful they are amidst
the mounting pile of shards.

Rosemerry Wahtola Trommer

Broken-ness is typically seen as a sign of falling apart. This poem reconfigures it as a way of becoming open. There is a world of difference. As we emerge from challenging journeys, we can often appreciate that what we feared was a breakdown was actually the start of a *breakthrough*.

Write about an aspect of your life that, in times past, you have tried to glue and tape back together.

- At what point did you stop trying to fix it, and what happened then?
- Is there anything you are trying very hard to patch up right now?
- In what areas of life have you loosened your grip and allowed something to emerge, and perhaps even flourish, beyond your control?
- What and where are your wildflowers?
- To what extent have you let go of a sense of urgency on your journeying?
- Are you more content to embrace life's natural unfolding?

Write about something to celebrate: the beauty of some aspect of your life, or a person you see and appreciate in a new way. This may come out as a poem. Let your writing lead you into joy.

> Clarify what is emerging

The Wild Iris

At the end of my suffering
there was a door.

Hear me out: that which you call death
I remember.

Overhead, noises, branches of the pine shifting.
Then nothing. The weak sun
flickered over the dry surface.

It is terrible to survive
as consciousness
buried in the dark earth.

Then it was over: that which you fear, being
a soul and unable
to speak, ending abruptly, the stiff earth
bending a little. And what I took to be
birds darting in low shrubs.

You who do not remember
passage from the other world
I tell you I could speak again: whatever
returns from oblivion returns
to find a voice:

from the center of my life came
a great fountain, deep blue
shadows on azure seawater.

Louise Gluck

This is the title poem in Louise Gluck's 1992 collection, which centres on a year's life in and around a garden. The flower-titled poems all speak in the voice of the flower, and make vivid the movement through death to regeneration in nature's life-cycle. The flowers are beautiful, but there is no pretty sentimentality about their journey through the seasons.

Here, the Wild Iris breaks through earth's surface again, telling the story it brings back from a winter 'buried in the dark earth'.

- Where does the flower's account resonate with your own experiences?
- What is 'the door' you have found beyond dark and difficult days?
- The Wild Iris became aware of the movement of earth and birds. What were the indicators of changing times for you?

The poem expresses the Wild Iris' shift from being silenced to the recovery of speech.

- Are you finding your voice in a new season?
- What is the story you want to communicate — to speak out, recount, declare, affirm or proclaim?

In the final lines, the Wild Iris comes into its own, as its rich, true colour pours forth.

- Where do you sense a fresh flourishing of the person you truly are?

Chapter 7: Resolving

Write in response to any of the above questions that resonate with you; you could either free-write in prose or in poetic lines of free verse, as in Gluck's poem. Let your words blossom and grow in the open air of the page.

> Celebrate calmer waters

Gift

A day so happy.
Fog lifted early, I worked in the garden.
Hummingbirds were stopping over honeysuckle flowers.
There was no thing on earth I wanted to possess.
I knew no one worth my envying him.
Whatever evil I had suffered, I forgot.
To think that once I was the same man did not embarrass me.
In my body I felt no pain.
When straightening up, I saw the blue sea and sails.

Czeslaw Milosz

There can be unexpected days where despite everything, all feels well with the world and ourselves. We cannot make them happen, only live in a way which welcomes their arrival as a gift of sheer grace. This poem celebrates such a day, in nine simple lines. Poet Anthony Wilson describes it as a 'hymn to letting go'.

The tone is settled and assured. The poem evokes a deep sense of peace and well-being. An integral part of this is what the Speaker is freed *from*: objects of envy, painful memories and physical pain itself.

Can you put words to such a day in your own life? It might be a very recent one, perhaps even in the midst of challenging times; or you may have a stand-out, golden day to which you return in memory and which still has the power to uplift you.

Write nine clear, simple statements, line by line, tracking the pattern of this poem. Your statements might note what you see, what you do, what is delightfully present — perhaps in the natural world, what is refreshingly absent, and/or how you feel in your being. The result will be your own

'Gift' poem; a snapshot of a special day, framed forever in a short, focussed piece. You may wish to refer back to the earlier poem that we looked at as we explored the reckoning process, and reflect on how it is different from this 'gift'. Are there any similarities?

> Find a way of marking the spot

Lost and Found

Things I have lost:
>A few umbrellas. I no longer carry one.
>A silver ring – three strands plaited, a pretty thing,
>>my very first.
>A poem sent to me by my friend.
>Some memories. Now, I don't know which ones they were.

And found:
>On Spiddal beach, among the stones, a pendant,
>>No chain attached, a fairy charm.
>Late at night, a bunch of carnations, fresh,
>>lying in the middle of our street.
>In Strandhill, on my loneliest day, a pebble
>>with the imprint of a long-gone sea shell.

Imelda Maguire

The poem assembles a collection of items lost and found. Those 'lost' are personally significant to the Speaker. Those 'found' link to others' lives and times, raising questions about the stories behind them.

What have you lost along your way? And what have you found? Take some moments to list these under two headings. Think about how these items link to an emotion or significant aspect of your own life. What makes their discovery or disappearance memorable? Perhaps there is something abstract, but no less real, that you have lost or found on your way — fear, trust, spontaneity, courage, faith…?

Shape your list into an order that pleases you, and follow the poet's example in adding a brief description, adjective or comment that hints at why they are memorable.

Chapter 7: Resolving

If you are feeling in a creative mood, you could take an item from Imelda Maguire's poem and tell its story:

- What happened to the silver ring — or an umbrella?
- Why was the bunch of carnations lying in the street?
- Who owned the pendant?

When you find yourself…	Writing may help you to…
• Seeing clearly the way one has come	• Clarify key marker points
• Drawing a line, even if short of ideal	• Note changes between then and now
• Facing the reality of a goal met	• Explore experience vs. expectation
• Sensing an endpoint in self/situation	• Explore indications of ending
• At peace in a new configuration	• Ground this new way of being
• Discerning the start of a new season	• Clarify what is emerging
• Feeling relieved and more settled	• Celebrate calmer waters
• Reaching or releasing your goal	• Find a way of marking the spot

Chapter 8: Reconstituting

- Integrating experiences
- More empathic of others' journeys
- Accepting who and where you are
- Telling a changed story
- With wiser self-knowledge
- Reviewing both inner and outer journey
- Reflecting on new insights
- Fully engaged with the present

'So what is it to be, Julia? Re-start or fresh start?' I was sitting in the Refectory of Chester Cathedral with Canon Jane, the Vice-Dean. With the Cathedral now fully reopened after the Covid lockdown, we were talking over coffee about what came next in my volunteer role as Poet-in-Residence.

'What's the difference?' I asked. 'Well,' she replied, 'Re-start is picking up what we did before. Fresh start is a blank sheet.' 'Fresh start, then,' I said, and immediately felt a sense of relief. I was not beholden to how things had been; there was permission to let go of prospective events that were planned but had to be postponed, and which had now lost momentum.

Reconstituting beyond the worst of the Covid-19 crisis has caused many to reflect on the way ahead. If the resolving process marks the final shift beyond what might have been, the reconstituting process establishes the steps of what might now become.

What do we wish to restore, perhaps with a new sense of its value? What needs readjusting? What do we want to leave behind, and what might we want to start? This process is multi-faceted, and takes an energy which many were surprised to find lacking in the season beyond lockdown. Where they expected to be running out to reclaim their former lives with joy, they have found themselves languishing. Reconstituting, it seems, is no quick fix.

In the last chapter, we reflected on how a sense of 'resolving' may emerge in layers. Yet, becoming gradually clearer about where we *are not* may still leave us uncertain about where we *are going*. There can be a sense of dislocation that makes it difficult to muster up the appetite to travel onward.

Energy may be low, as we realise just how much has changed within us and around us since our journey began. Covid-19 has proven to be a portal into a new world, one that is bringing us further challenging problems to contend with: international conflicts; cost of living; climate change. Some did not come out of lockdown with us. The rest of us have emerged that bit older, and affected in various ways by that unprecedented time.

Some losses are hard to pin down. When myself and my husband were burgled a few years ago, it was not just the stolen jewellery that was distressing. Gone, too, was a sense of security in our own home. Such intangible losses can make a real impact on day-to-day living. Identifying and expressing them is important. The reconstituting process involves making space to acknowledge what is never coming back.

Perhaps one loss that needs naming is that of *capacity*. For many, Covid-19's legacy was a reduced personal 'bandwidth'; people no longer had the capacity to sustain everything they were doing before. This might also be true for those emerging from a significant period of ill-health. And those recovering from burn-out may need to re-balance a previous overload of capacity that led to their problems in the first place.

In a world where we can feel we should be fully productive and firing on all cylinders, 24/7 (and perhaps expect that of ourselves), accepting our finite, human limitations can be challenging. But embracing this reality, without self-recrimination, is a compassionate way of nurturing ourselves that makes the most of the energy we *do* have. We may even move from FOMO (Fear of Missing Out) to JOMO (Joy of Missing Out).

When our own world has undergone a profound shaking, it looks different in the aftermath. The reconstitution process lends it a new shimmer. In good times, this reminds us that the present moment holds no guarantee of permanence. When times are tough, it reminds us that these days too will pass. It is a shimmer that sparkles with light; the consolations, connection, purpose and hope that we have found to sustain us through our various ups and downs, gleam along our way. They are constants that hold us steady — trusted practices, purposes and person(s) that help us simply to keep walking, occasional stumbles notwithstanding.

As energy is renewed, the reconstituting process releases it outwards into fresh, creative purposes. It is the sort of energy that draws some people to campaign for justice or champion an issue that has been at the heart of their pain. Such people include Brigitte Chaudry, who founded RoadPeace — the UK charity supporting those affected by road crashes — after her own son, Mansoor, was killed by a red-light offender in 1990. She wanted to address the injustices and lack of compassion she experienced in the wake of such personal tragedy. By integrating her experience in a way that is fruitful both personally and for the community, Brigitte moved beyond defining herself as another victim of this terrible incident.

Reconstituting completes the unwanted journey's cycle. It integrates all we have salvaged for good, through the preceding processes: all we have learned about ourselves — strengths, assumptions, pressure points and how to nurture ourselves. When we meet our next unwanted journey — and we will — we are more equipped to navigate it smoothly.

In comparing my arthritis journey to my earlier pathway of involuntary infertility, I find myself more able to confront my difficult days and particular pitfalls; more able to preserve a perspective that prevents this journey from being all-consuming. I also recognise the need to live in compassionate partnership with my body.

In the unwanted journey's final turn, we catch up with ourselves, to settle into our new way of living, one step at a time. It is a hopeful and calmer process, one that essentially looks forward rather than back, and with an altered perspective.

The French novelist Proust writes about the real journey being the capacity to see the same landscape with changed eyes, and poet T S Eliot notes that at the end of all our journeying, we arrive back where we started, but 'know the place for the first time'.

The author Arthur J Frank — who wrote about his brush, first with a heart attack and then with cancer — reflects that if a patient emerges from cancer the same as they went into it, the illness has not done its work. Within the challenge of the illness, he asserts, lies a hidden opportunity to come into a different way of being.

What once felt so alienating can, itself, become a rich point of connection. Having experienced feeling powerless in the face of loss, we may emanate a natural empathy for another's story of personal pain. This is something that can be immediately sensed, even unconsciously. Somehow, others know that we 'get it'. This is so, even as our own hurts have softened.

Reconstituting is the season when our present life becomes fully absorbing, and we are no longer pre-occupied with how things might have been or how they actually were. We are able to recall our journey without re-experiencing it. As L P Hartley writes in his novel *The Go-Between*, 'The past is another country. They do things differently there.'

It is worth taking time to cherish any unexpected treasures that have emerged from our journey as we have engaged with it. What is coming into the space left when what you had was taken away? There may be a new direction in life, new relationships and/or a new quality to relationships. There may be internal changes, too, of outlook, purpose and character. These are not compensations for your loss, but they can be welcomed as consolations. The intrusion of Covid-19 forced unwanted journeys upon all who lived through it, often acting as a catalyst for issues previously hidden or ignored. In one fell swoop, Covid swept away many of everyday life's fixtures and fittings to reveal things that needed to be addressed.

During Covid-19, I became more Chester Cathedral's Poet-in-Exile than Poet-in-Residence. This put a halt to plans for some ambitious poetry-based events I was working on in early 2020. As lockdown ended, I realised I had been setting these up out of an 'ought' rather than an enthusiasm. Some of those involved in helping me organise this project were no longer in post, and I had no heart for a restart.

Reconstituting has meant honestly facing that, alongside my own writing, my energy flows more naturally in encouraging small groups to engage with poetry than in master-minding big events. Beyond Covid lockdown, it has led many to make significant shifts in their way of life. It changed attitudes to work in general or to a job in particular. It inspired some to pay more serious attention to caring for their well-being. Relationships have ended, started, or radically changed. More space has been made for the 'passion projects' so often put on hold.

Reconstituting can feel like turning life over to a fresh, blank page. As we seek to establish our steps in new territory, writing can help us to map our way. On the page, we can name what has gone and sharpen our awareness of what is around us now, as we explore what to weave into our fresh start. We can chart steps we are taking day by day, and discern emerging patterns as we look back over what we have been writing.

Reviewing our Writing

As we settle into a regular personal writing practice, our journals start to fill and we accumulate material to look back on. We may resist re-reading our journal, but regularly reviewing our writing is not wallowing in the past — it can deepen our insight in the present and offer useful pointers for future action. It has been said that we may learn more about ourselves from re-reading our journals than writing them. Even an immediate re-reading helps us see our writing with a fresh eye; we can spot what we were not aware of earlier, especially in a piece of free-writing.

When we re-read after a longer gap, our greater level of detachment from what is on the page may help us notice even more. One way to do this is to build in a weekly review.

The simplest approach is to read through your week's journal entries, noting what feels significant and writing some follow-up reflections on what you find. You may pick up on a recurring theme: achievements to celebrate, issues to explore, progress — or not — on what matters to you, and an indication of intentions to set for the week ahead.

My own approach is to start with some preliminary free-writing, to gain a feel for the week as a whole, before digging into the detail. For a while I used the prompt: 'What have I done?', to encourage myself. My reviewing had lapsed into a dispiriting litany of all the ways I had fallen short of the goals I had set myself. I decided to regain momentum by writing what I *had* done, rather than what I *had not*. This was more affirming, and helped me view myself with greater kindness. I could see how, if I had neglected one area, it was often because I had been moving forward in another.

I added a second prompt: 'What have I heard?' This helped me recall incidents, issues or words that had caught my attention and stayed with me beyond the moment. I would fill a page, and then re-read this writing alongside my week's journal entries, matching my overall impressions against the day-by-day specifics; this helped me separate things passing from those with a more lasting impact. Sometimes, the smallest incident punches a significance well above its weight.

Your personal journey will have its own questions and priorities; directions to be set and values nurtured. You may prefer to review your journal fortnightly, monthly or quarterly.

You may change your approach from season to season, adapting it to the needs of the time. You could set your own weekly free-writing prompt:

- What has felt important?
- What have I learned and who have been my teachers?
- What has sustained me and/or drained me?
- What am I grateful for?
- How have I navigated the unexpected?

Deciding beforehand how you will structure your approach with the same weekly prompt(s) also helps with motivation: you know exactly what you are going to do when you pick up your pen.

As you re-read your journal, you may notice certain issues keep cropping up. This is not necessarily cause for dismay. Writing something down re-centres our intentions and fosters accountability in following them through. It can underline our values and remind us of priorities we may have let slip. It can offer insight about where we are vulnerable and help us monitor our progress over the long haul. Your revisiting of an issue may be a valuable resetting of attention on an important area, as you persist in moving forward.

Of course, some journal entries recycle the same old issues to avoid facing what is difficult. If you discern that this is going on, a free-writing prompt such as, 'What is this really about?' or 'As I look beneath this writing, I see…' might help to explore it. But let the pen act as a compassionate, as well as honest, friend. In areas where we struggle, the oft-quoted advice to 'be curious, not furious' applies.

If you feel stuck, you can shift your approach to writing about what makes taking action difficult. What keeps getting in the way — really? You can write about what you most value; about what would come up for you if you decided not to act; or about the times you acted despite your fears, and how that worked out. You can break down an overwhelming task into smaller, practical steps, or identify supportive resources — including your own strengths and experience.

Alongside this, it can be helpful to amass material you can draw on for writing prompts at a later date. This could include your own well-being armoury of quotations and conversational comments; inspiring poems and wise words as resources for when you wonder what to write about. Your journal becomes your unique self-help manual, challenging you beyond your comfort zone; allowing you to cut yourself some slack.

This ultimately faces us with another issue: what do we do long-term with our growing shelf of full journals? Keep, or get rid? What would happen to them if anything were to happen to us? Who would get to read them? Those whom we have written about?

One journaller I know has an occasional bonfire where she burns her old journals. She sees it as a ritual that marks how her life has moved on. Her journals have done their work and she can let them go. The difference they have made lives on in her. If this does not appeal, you may want to ask a trusted person to oversee your journals' destruction when you are past being able to do it yourself.

In re-reading my journals from long ago, I have discovered how much they expressed strong emotions at a time very different from now; I do not feel a need to keep this writing. In fact, too deep a re-reading starts to stir my feelings up to the point of re-living what has long been left behind. I chose to file some extracts I have selected to keep and let go of the rest. More recent journals are closer to my current experience; I still want to be able to refer back to them. As I have developed a wider range of journalling approaches, they have become a more useful resource. For now, at least, I am keeping them.

Debbie's Story: Writing to Keep, Writing to Release

Debbie and her husband Jonathan's[1] lives changed forever in July 2012, when Jonathan suffered a brain haemorrhage and Debbie became his primary carer over his two-year recovery period. As critical illness overturned their everyday working lives, the couple realised how isolated they were. With immediate family living at a distance and overseas, it

---

[1] Names changed

seemed they were on their own. Help came in the form of neighbours, their GP, and charities such as Headway and The Brain Charity in Liverpool. The couple were resourced through these connections; especially vital at times when Jonathan was at home and could not be left.

Initially, Debbie was on auto-pilot, working long hours and caring for her husband, but as the emotions of her situation began to surface, she found herself picking up her pen. 'I wrote whenever my feelings were overwhelming,' she says. 'My writing was a stream of consciousness about how I felt in that moment. It helped release some of the power out of the strong emotion.'

As it did so, Debbie's writing naturally took a more reflective turn, enabling a shift of perspective. 'Writing my thoughts on paper helped me make sense of what happened,' she says.

Debbie took things further by attending some well-being writing workshops and courses. Although she kept what she wrote in these sessions, she destroyed the rest of her personal writing. She says this has been a cathartic process in itself. Debbie did not just write about her losses; she also expressed gratitude for the gift of Jonathan's life and their life together. 'It's a life transformed,' Debbie says; she and Jonathan did not merely survive their unwanted journey — their 'reconstituted' selves are completely different from how they were before.

Jonathan's memory loss of events before his haemorrhage has closed the door on much of his old life, but Debbie notices some positive differences in him, as he gradually returned to full-time work. 'He has let go of others' judgements,' she says, 'and I believe that as a direct consequence of this, he has soared in his career beyond where he ever thought he would be.'

Her life has changed, too: inspired to help others, as she had been helped, she started volunteering and then took a basic counselling course. One thing led to another and she eventually become a full-time bereavement counsellor. Her life now centres around different values. Stepping back from former busyness, she has re-set her priorities around compassion, kindness and having more time for others, believing that these things are too important to ignore.

'I try to show myself more compassion and empathy so that I can support and be more empathic towards others. My life somehow now feels more aligned. I wouldn't undo these changes even if I could.'

What Debbie wrote:

(At a writing workshop, Debbie was asked to write freely from any line in Derek Walcott's poem, *Love after Love*. She chose: 'You will love again the stranger who was yourself.')

'In time I will come to connect to myself as I am and not another's ideal of me. I will learn to leave the pre-haemorrhage Jonathan behind and live with the new "Jonathan", which requires me to step-up, be more independent and venture out into new surroundings which admittedly makes me uncomfortable. My reliance on the "old Jonathan" has come to an end. I must say goodbye to the "old Jonathan" and welcome the few, rare, and cherished moments "old Jonathan" comes to visit.

'I will always be grateful to the "old Jonathan" that loved me and cared for me in every aspect of life. "Old Jonathan" helped me to face many adversities, to become better than I could ever imagine and move towards the person I wanted to be, the person I am becoming.

'Thank you to the "old Jonathan" for supporting me through those difficulties. Now the time has come to face future difficult moments and adversities alone.'

In the Reconstituting process, writing may help you to:

- Reflect fruitfully on your path here
- Clarify renewed beliefs and priorities
- Celebrate gains beyond the losses
- Establish your new narrative
- Better manage your internal world
- Discern your line of travel
- Embrace what to take forward
- Maintain your life's momentum

Journalling Suggestions

> Reflect fruitfully on your path here

Walled Garden Writing

Someone in remission for cancer once described her life to me as like a 'walled garden'.

With her diagnosis, it felt as though the walls had closed in, constricting growth, and with no prospect of seasons to come. As her treatment completed and she came into remission, the walls moved outward again. 'There is space and time to grow things,' she said, 'but the walls are still there. The space has its limits.'

Walled gardens are all different. Some are geometrically ordered, with neat pathways; others more wild and abundant. They may boast exotic plants, beautiful flowers, a variety of vegetables and fruit. They may have a glasshouse or orangery, fountain or pond, statues and benches. Whenever I visit one, there is always something fresh to notice...

Picture your own life as a walled garden, and write about how things are in *this* season.

- What is old and dying?
- What new shoots and buds are appearing?
- What has begun to flourish, perhaps surprisingly?
- Are there any bare patches of earth?

In your mind's eye, take a stroll around. What tasks need your attention?

- Is there pruning to be done?
- What needs to be planted, or uprooted and the ground dug over?
- What needs watering and supporting?
- What just needs to be left to flourish naturally?
- What might it mean to sit and simply savour your surroundings?

Reflect on these questions and write some gardener's notes in response. How do these transpose into actions you might want to take in your life?

This is an exercise you can come back to, as you inspect, and reflect on, your garden in another season. You might combine it with making a visit to a walled garden in your neighbourhood.

> Clarify renewed beliefs and priorities

Past and Present Beliefs

All of us hold beliefs about different aspects of life. They may be beliefs about the world, God, other people; about what is important; about the future, about life and death; even about ourselves. Our beliefs affect how we approach challenging times, and such times may bring to the surface unconscious beliefs and assumptions we were not fully aware we held.

Significant experiences put our beliefs to the test. Some will be strengthened, others reshaped; some will be lost, others found. Reflect on the beliefs that guide and inform you on your way through life. How have these been refined or re-made in the light of your journey? Think back to an earlier time and write for ten minutes on the prompt, 'I used to believe that…' You can free-write, or if you prefer, use the list or mind map format to gather material. Put down whatever comes to mind, however wide-ranging the beliefs that emerge.

When you have done this, write again from the prompt: 'I now believe that…'

Use the same format as you did for your first writing response. You might wish to include a section that covers 'I still believe that…'

Re-read what you have written and write some reflective sentences on what you have noticed. Consider what beliefs you most hold dear and what has prompted some to change. How have those that remain survived or been strengthened by your experiences?

How do you feel as you look at what you currently believe?

> Celebrate gains beyond the losses

If Only/And Yet

Though we all have events or experiences in our lives that we wish had been different, as we start to accept these things and live through them, we can discover that these losses are softened by some consolatory gains. For example:

'If only…' [my daughter had not married an Australian and gone to live in Sydney]

'And yet…' [I now have an international family and have visited a part of the world I would not otherwise have gone to.]

Set up two columns for two lists. Head the first column 'If Only', and the second, 'And Yet'. Under the first column, write down things you wish could have been different. Be as specific as you can.

Now move across to the second column. Can you add an 'And Yet' that counter-balances each 'If Only'? It may not outweigh it, but it is important to acknowledge the elements that form part of the bigger, fuller picture of the journey we have been on.

> Establish your new narrative

Taking Hold of Our Story

Setting down an experience in words helps us form a coherent account of it. We have to make decisions about how to order our events; how we make sense of our actions and reactions; what is most important and what is incidental; how we interpret the actions of others. But the story we tell ourselves, and others about ourselves, is not static. It changes as we navigate events, learn more about what is going on within and without, find ourselves in a different relationship with things that have happened and people involved, and notice our feelings and outlook shifting. We know when we have changed, because our story has changed. We can also observe the opposite in those stuck in an old story, and locked into attitudes that close them off to other possibilities.

What is the story of your journey in the process of reconstitution? How has your experience impacted your attitudes, outlook, insights and action? Reflect on your current journey, or one from further back in the past, and write your story as you wish to tell it now. What changes do you notice in your take on things if you compare this with how you have written and/or talked about it in the past?

When they see how things have changed, people sometimes choose to let go of the old journal entries they have moved on from, getting rid of earlier writing as a symbol of walking free of an outgrown life. What do you want to do?

Poetry Explorations

> Better manage your internal world

Writing to My Self

Attending only to the words dropping from my head onto the page must be swift
Before the editor inside my head shouts
Cut!
Delete!
Eggs me on instead to skirt over,
Flee in flagrant flight from the real
GUTS of my words.
Hear me, I plead to the page (ignoring that editor weighing down on my left shoulder),
I am here, telling you that sometimes I feel like I'm living on
JUPITER. I'm an entire planet apart,
Kitted out in a skin that needs shedding,
Lizard-like in outer space, looking, longing, for some kind of sign… or a
Message – for what? Maybe I'm expecting incoming
News from the firmament, that will
Open up new
Possibilities, or a kind voice over the airways lobbing me a
QUESTION:
Remember? it will ask me, *remember your TRUE*
Self?
The one beneath that skin, the one
Underneath all that shiny
Veneer? She has always been there. She is always there.
Watch and listen. Can you see how she is no
Xerox copy of anybody else? She can only be

YOU! Enjoy the ride, this is your
Zig-zag journey around the orbit of your planet. Live it well!

Anne-Marie Smith

We return to the alphabet poem introduced earlier in the book, with all the challenge, fun and surprising insight it can bring; I make no apologies for its re-appearance. Repeating an exercise invariably yields something new, however familiar the form.

This alphabet poem is an honest exploration of the Speaker's internal dialogue, as they sit down to write at depth. In italicised speech, it brings to life the interaction of three distinct voices: the Speaker's Core Self, their Inner Editor and their Wise Self. The Inner Editor's brusque interruption is all too familiar, but it is the nurturing voice of the Wise Self that has the last and more powerful word. Containing these disparate parts within the alphabet poem form underlines that they are parts of one cogent and whole person.

Many of us would identify with having an inner conversation. The reconstituting process is not one in which we have silenced these voices, but one where we possess the self-awareness to recognise them. We are able to detach ourselves to hear and evaluate the messages these voices bring as we decide what to take note of and what to dismiss. What inner dialogues are activated in you as you sit down to write? Can you identify these various voices? Take a moment to reflect. Note down the sort of things they say, and perhaps identify each one with a name or label. Though we could spend time reflecting on where they originated, it is more fruitful to recognise and manage them when they make their presence known day-to-day.

Create your own alphabet poem that explores your own inner dialogue and the choices you want to make to navigate through it. You may prefer to change writing form and set out these inner voices like characters in play, or as a short story, where they gather around a table and talk with one another. Or you may wish to change subject, and use the alphabet form to explore another aspect of your writing, such as the rituals, routines and rhythms in how you go about it.

> Discern your line of travel

Restricted Living

I have lived restricted
for so many years
the days they vanish
the years disappear
One day I feel
from the ocean a breeze
It warms my inside
and melts my ice
There are doors forgotten
that lead somewhere
though I never dared
believe they existed

Kjell Walfridsson

Poet Mark Strand observes that, 'Poetry is about slowing down. You sit and you read something, you read it again, and it reveals a little bit more, and things come to light that you could never have predicted.'

There is much to reflect on in this short, but profound, poem. So take some time to allow yourself and your own journey to inhabit it. A good way to do this is by reading the poem slowly — perhaps aloud — several times. Let your mind rest, without analysing the words. Let them be and simply resonate as they will. On repeated readings, be open to the particular line, phrase or image that nudges for your attention. Let it suggest itself to you as a prompt for your own writing.

When you are ready, write this line at the top of your page. It may become the first of other lines you add underneath it, creating your own poem. Or you may prefer to use it as the prompt for a piece of free-writing. Remember to re-read what you have written to see what 'things come to light' for you in this process.

> Embrace what you take forward

You Do Not Need Another Self-Help Book

Just get up from your desk
and open the window,
keep silent until you hear three
sounds you've never heard before,
run your tongue around your mouth,
smell the air.
I tell you what, put down this book
and do this one thing now:
let your hands drift out and touch,
then drift again;
run your fingers
over rough wood, then let them fall
against your own soft skin. I met a woman once
who told me to touch her jumper,
Expensive, she said. It bobbled
under my hand so she told me
I wasn't feeling it right,
and for too long I believed her
because she said quality spoke.
I didn't see how beautiful
the world is
with its only wish
that I belong,
and how my touch,
my smell, hearing, sight,
so different from hers
is the only one that matters.

Sarah Salway

In this poem, the Speaker starts with the 'help' and ends with the 'self', moving from instruction, to a reminder to have confidence in personal insight. Rather than following another's lead and absorbing their worldview, there is a time to trust one's own direct, unmediated experience.

The poem's title and first lines wryly present the sort of instructions it purports to dismiss, but you may like to try them out. Leave this book and engage each of your senses with some aspect of your present surroundings. Write down what you experience as a short poem, perhaps taking a line for each sense.

Who or what has been your equivalent of the pushy woman in the pricey pullover? Write about a time when you were being pressured to take on board a way of seeing the world you have now left behind. How did you feel about this then… and now?

The 'quality' that speaks to the jumper-wearer is financial value, but the Speaker is more in tune with qualities of beauty and connection. What are the qualities that speak to you?

What are the values and insights that you want to cherish? Write a poem or a set of sentences that each start with: 'What matters most to me is…'

> Strengthen contentment in process

My Jigsawed Life

rumbles in its box like a rattle of dry bones.
I scan fragments, see random parts — petal,
foot, bird-wing, half a windowpane,
unbroken wash of cobalt sky.
But first I feel for edges, find a frame.

I stir a whirlpool of disconnected
amber roof tiles, white boat-hull, cobbles.
I pile colours into tribes, hold
each piece in loving attention,
interlock each hand with its neighbour.

Life reveals itself, piece by slow piece.
When I can find no more people,
and turn my eye towards clouds,
suddenly every piece I touch
is alive with arms, legs, faces.

Boats are anchored, trees weighted with leaves.
I develop a joiner's eye.
Trust in a piece for each gap,
Slops of blue-green waves
flow into a swathe of sea.

I thought it the work of a day, a week,
but it continues as the picture fills.
Blocks of bright-coloured houses
fall into line, form a water-front.

Julia McGuinness

Underlying this poem is the concept that assembling life's pieces has similarities with putting together a jigsaw. Each process involves setting boundaries, sustaining a focus, seeking connections and trusting that the gaps will eventually be filled even if there is no obvious piece that immediately fits.

Working on a large jigsaw entails being patient and engaged with the process, one area at a time. As in life, if we try to attend to everything at once, we end up not getting very far with anything. But this slowness opens up a tender familiarity with all its parts, in a detail that goes much deeper than a passing glance at the image on the box. In a reconstituting process, we are content not to push the pace.

- To what extent do you resonate with any of the poem's life/jigsaw connections?
- Where has it been important to set some boundaries to 'find a frame'?
- If you were to put your life into tribes of colour, what would those colours be?
- Have you ever given up the search for something, then found it coming naturally across your path when your attention was somewhere else?
- How do you live with a gap, trusting there will be a piece to fill it at some point?

Write a response to these questions and any further links that occur to you. Do these suggest a different way of approaching some area in your life?

Chapter 8: Reconstituting

Perhaps you have a particular pastime or activity — sport, skill or art — that you practise. What connections can you make between this and the way you live your life? Write about these, as a poem or a free-writing reflection. Are there ways you approach this task that you could creatively transpose to another area of life?

When you find yourself…	Writing may help you to…
• Integrating experiences	• Reflect fruitfully on your path here
• More empathic of others' journeys	• Clarify beliefs and priorities
• Accepting who and where you are	• Celebrate gains beyond losses
• Telling a changed story	• Establish your new narrative
• With wiser self-knowledge	• Better manage your internal world
• Reviewing your inner and outer journey	• Discern your line of travel
• Reflecting on new insights	• Embrace what to take forward
• Fully engaged with the present	• Strengthen contentment in process

Writing the Journeys We Never Wanted to Make

Chapter 9: Relapsing

- Angry at unfairness, comparing with others
- Overwhelmed by a setback
- Feeling you are re-tracking old ground
- With old reactions surfacing
- With best efforts exhausted
- Angry at self for not moving on

When I told people about this book and described the processes I am presenting, I was met with nods of recognition. But when I added that, of course, I would be noting the process of relapsing, the nods were accompanied by relieved, affirming sighs.

It would be wonderful to think that we tracked our journey in a seamless glide from one process to the next, passing the finishing line with a neatly completed tick box of lessons learned, job done. But human beings do not advance in a steady, linear fashion. Motivation and energy levels fluctuate from day to day. We are not in control of the circumstances and events that life brings us. Difficulties can be like buses: no sign of trouble for ages and then everything comes down the road towards us at once. The sky-high electricity bill comes in; we have toothache and cannot get a dental appointment; and then something said in casual conversation hits a raw nerve.

Before we know it, our mood plummets. We can become tired, which makes it harder to summon up the energy to follow through our intentions. So we drift into the doldrums. As someone in this state once told me: 'I don't feel as though I am in any process at all just now. I'm floating a round in the middle, lost.'

The pathway through Covid-19 was riddled with disruptions, as the in/out backdrop of lockdown shifted in ways over which we had little control. The feeling of being stuck indoors forever, with freedom dangled out of reach, brought down many a mood, leading to a quick comfort fix — expanding waistlines, alongside a growing weariness. As the proverb puts it, 'Hope deferred makes the heart sick'; and a sick heart can be tempted to throw in the towel.

Relapsing is a process in itself, and we need the courage to confront it with compassion. More often than not, the walk to well-being takes two steps forward, one step back. None of us are strangers to an experience of relapsing. But being in this process is less important than how we respond to where we are. Acknowledging what has happened and seeking a constructive pathway through can minimise the impact of our stumble along the way. Relapse does not have to mean collapse.

There are three ways we can engage when we find ourselves in 'relapse territory': We can rage at how we have let things get so out of hand, berating ourselves for our failure to manage amid life's challenges. The inner talk in our minds spills onto the pages of our journal, peppering it with 'oughts' and 'shoulds'. But a plant does not grow better for being shouted at; if we put ourselves at the mercy of our critical Inner Bully, we will feel even more defeated. We need to find a language and a way of kindness towards ourselves, which is not the same as being indulgent.

Learning how to manage ourselves — when to encourage ourselves to step up, and when to cut ourselves some slack — is a life-skill. Relapse offers an opportunity for some practice. When we struggle to get to grips with talking kindly to ourselves, it can help to reflect on how we would speak to a friend in our position. Words of compassion and encouragement often come more naturally when we are dealing with someone else. The challenge is to re-direct this talk towards ourselves. What would it feel like to do this?

A second option is to ruminate about where we are, tracking the same ground over and over, wishing it could have been different and lamenting how we have ended up. But such repetition only works us further into a rut. We become prone to being overwhelmed, losing our sense of perspective and our hope with it. We cannot afford to expend our energies in reliving the past and becoming paralysed with regrets. It is time to turn our attention to the present moment, the only place where we have agency to make a change that will move us towards a different future, one step at a time, however small.

Our third option, then, is to review where we are in a spirit of non-critical curiosity. Calm reviewing, rather than compulsive reliving, is more helpful in taking us forward. We might write freely in response to prompts such as: 'What has happened to bring me here?' or 'What needs did I have that were calling for my particular attention, and how did I respond?' Past journal entries may also harbour clues to our route — perhaps even in what we *did not* write, as well as what we did. Our aim is to make a fair appraisal of what has led us to this point, an appraisal both compassionate and truthful.

Nothing is wasted. Reflecting on relapsing can yield valuable insights. It can also suggest what we might do to look after ourselves more effectively, to strengthen our strategies for prevention before we slip into needing a cure. We may feel we are back at square one, but we are not: our experience offers us the opportunity to glean new information about our vulnerabilities and blind spots. We may discover that we have more options than we realised.

One evening, my journalling group agreed to spend a session re-reading and reviewing their journals. In the group feedback, several were surprised at how often they had been writing around the same issues, as particular personal themes and issues recurred time and again... At first there was some dismay but then we realised that engaging repeatedly with the same issue does not necessarily mean we are encountering it at the same level. To draw on an image from the poetry of T S Eliot, we can be moving up a spiral staircase.

We all have core concerns that form part of our unique, personal landscape; whether from our circumstances, particular outlook, upbringing or experience. There are elements of our lives that we may never eradicate or solve, but from which we gain a greater facility in managing as we circle and ascend the spiral. Challenging journeys can serve us by accelerating these turns, fast-tracking the wisdom we need to live life to its fullest.

It is also worth being aware of how we are repeating material in our journals. Repetition in our journals can be about re-setting rather than ruminating. I find that writing around my core values again from time to time — especially at the start of the year — is a way of realigning myself to my personal priorities. It acts both as a reminder and springboard to explore how to put what matters to me into practice in a new season.

The relapsing process is part of the journey, but need not mark its end, even when we are tempted to panic and sabotage the progress we have made. If our car develops one flat tyre, we do not deflate the other three and park ourselves at the side of the road. We deal with the problem tyre. In the same way, we need to keep our stumbles in perspective. Writing is a valuable way of helping us slow down to take stock, dispassionately, of just what has fallen apart, without turning an issue into a catastrophe. The page can be a place to identify options for moving forward. Relapse is only the end of the road if we choose to give up.

Writing to Re-engage

Once, we did not keep a journal. Then we discovered the value and the pleasure of putting words on the page. Yet now that has stopped — we have not written for some time and we fear that our journalling has lost its way. How can we get back on track?

Rather than pack your bags for a guilt trip, it is time to sit down with some self-compassion. Real life, for human beings, is rarely a problem-free run. You grow by navigating the ups and downs. Your writing may have hit a bit of a stumbling block, but even if you feel it has fallen into a total relapse, you are not back at square one. The writing experience you now have ushers you to the next turn upwards on a spiral staircase, rather than re-tracking old ground.

There are reasons why you are no longer journalling. It may be a creative pause from a practice that has become stale and needs some refreshment; perhaps an intentional break has somehow drifted into a longer one? What else has been going on in your life?

Some people stop writing in the good times; others stop when things are not so good. Life events — unexpected crises, changes of circumstances — can upend a regular rhythm of writing and knock it off-course. Let yourself be as you are. This could be an opportunity to bring your journalling into a rich, new phase.

Moving from relapsing towards renewal may mean returning to that first question in Chapter 1: *why do you want to write?* As you change, so may your reasons for writing. What you need from a journal now may be different from what was important then. You can revisit the other journalling questions, too. If your daily living patterns have changed, availability and energy levels may suggest a different time to write. Perhaps a different place would help? Do you need to try some fresh writing techniques or approaches? And as you change, the 'who' that is writing the journal shifts, too.

Take it gently in renewing a journalling habit. Be patient when you are living with difficult and tiring emotions such as weariness or grieving — and do not force the pace. Be realistic and commit to what, for you, would be the least ambitious amount of journalling to make a difference; the week when you complete the three journal entries that you set yourself, as opposed to only the three that you managed — after aiming to write daily — is much more likely to support your onward momentum.

Keeping journalling simple will also help make it sustainable. You could start with some postcard journalling: take just ten minutes to jot down something about what you see and sense around you, and about where you are — in whatever way you want to interpret that. Write no more than you could send on a postcard.

You could try some 'shimmer journalling'. Write a few lines about the particular moment, incident or experience in the day that has 'shimmered' in some way for you: a beautiful sunrise, a friend's kind words, that leaking tap finally fixed...

List journalling is also an accessible way of picking up on a journalling practice. Re-deploy your shopping list skills to create lists of whatever makes you smile, for instance: favourite pieces of music, hills climbed, places you have visited — or would like to. You could widen this to list the things you have been doing instead of journalling; of why it is okay to be where you are now; of reasons why you want to journal — or the things you do to avoid it. If all else fails, you could even write a list of what you *do not* feel like writing about.

Even if it feels like starting completely from scratch, take some time to review your former journalling practice. What was working well for you? What might you want to carry forward into this new phase?

When it comes to picking up the pen, do you want simply to turn to the next page in your former journal, or make a fresh start in a brand new book? If the latter, you may wish to make a final entry in your old journal in the form of a parting letter, thanking it for its company and telling it about your moving on.

Refresh your journal writing by getting experimental; try an approach or exercise you have never tried before, perhaps even one you have resisted or dismissed. Reflect on what comes up for you if you *refuse* to let yourself write in your journal. Do you start itching to put some words down?

Some accountability may help, too. Schedule a short writing slot in your diary or arrange to write with others, either online or face-to-face. Take your journal on a date to a local beauty spot or cafe, and write in it when you are there.

Ultimately, your journal is for you, not the other way round. It is there to help you explore writing in ways that will enhance your living with words. When it starts to become more chore than joy, it is a practice that needs refreshing.

Joanne's Story: Writing to Break a Deadlock

Joanne's father died in 2001, aged 71. She shed tears at the time, but wept on his birthday every succeeding year. On the day when he would have been 90, she found herself standing at the kitchen sink with tears running down her face, yet again. She says: 'It seemed that the same old emotion was coming up year after year and I thought, "I'm fed up of this." I went and sat straight down at my computer. I'd never previously written about my Dad. But I needed to clear my head and somehow purge myself. And, though I'm generally quite a private person, I felt compelled to share what I'd written with my Facebook friends.

'I was his pride and joy as a little girl, but at an early age I saw him for what he was — a flawed human being. I could do no wrong, but my brother could do no right! I remember awful dinner times as he watched for my brother to step out of line, my mother watching him, and me, invisible.

'I thought I was going to write a long rant about all the wrong things he had done that he shouldn't have. But as I wrote, I began thinking about the positives that he also gave me. I always knew that these were there, but I felt that the writing was giving me a choice.

'I could continue down a negative route, that I might later regret, or I could underline the positives that he'd given me. I could acknowledge that I am proud of these — and proud of him. Somehow, the writing helped me come to terms with my Dad and balance things in my head. I could let go of negatives and leave the past behind. It was very cathartic. Even posting this for others to read felt right.

'As I posted it I felt a sense of freedom. Comments came in from those who had never known my Dad, saying that he sounded like a lovely dad. I made no further responses or comments after I'd posted the piece. He had a passion for forensics and would read up about it. It's an area he would have loved to work in, if he'd not left school at thirteen. He had unfulfilled dreams.'

Joanne found that this piece of writing impacted her own dream life: 'I used to have difficult dreams about my father, in which I was still angry with him. But these have largely gone since I did the writing. You can make a big shift a long time after an event, and you don't have to force it either. It will come up when it needs to.'

In the Relapsing process, writing may help you to :

- Re-claim your own unique journey
- Identify priorities and recover momentum
- Turn the circle into a spiral staircase
- Deepen understanding of your choices
- Find some anchorage for a reset
- Find self-compassion and forgiveness

Journalling Suggestions

> Re-claim your own unique journey

Writing by Numbers

The relapsing process can feel overwhelming, and the task of getting back into a creative rhythm like having a big hill to climb, especially when others seem to be striding around on the summit; but comparison is toxic. The only constructive way of scoring is on our own scale.

The structured journalling template below may help you clarify aspects of your own situation and find some immediate steps forward on your own unique journey. In each case, write the number you would put against each question, and then free-write for a few sentences on those that follow.

On a scale of 1-10, where '10' is the best it can be and '0' is the worst:

* What number reflects how you are today? Write about what makes it that choice. What feelings, thoughts, behaviours or circumstances landed you there?

* What number would reflect how you were before you dropped into the relapsing process? Write about the difference. How does this make you feel? What did you have going for you that suggested its higher score?

* Now, write about the factors you identify as bringing that pre-relapse score down (internal, external, or both). Have these something to teach you about how you might prevent this drop, rather than having to pick up the pieces afterwards?

* Write the number that is one *down* from how you are now. Write about what stops today's score being that number (a minus number is allowed for this!).

* Write the number that is one *up* from where you are now. Write about what would enable that to become today's number for you.

* Finally, in the light of your last answer, write about any choices you can make now to help you step out in an upward direction. If what needs to happen to raise the score is an event out of your control, is there a shift of mind-set, a letting go, that is in your remit to make a difference?

> Identify priorities and recover momentum

Five Small Stones

The Biblical story of David and Goliath is familiar to many. Giant Goliath was the arrogant champion of the terrifying Philistine army — their ultimate weapon, whom it seemed impossible to defeat. Yet David, a simple shepherd-boy armed only with faith, courage and a sling with five smooth stones, overcame him.

When we relapse, we can feel small and overwhelmed in the face of forces ranged against us. This is a time to go back to basics.

Use your journal each morning to identify your five smooth stones of the day. What are the key tasks, affirmations to remember, or one-off actions to rebuild a habit, that you could do? Write each one down. You will do many other useful things over the day, but these are the key ones needed to help move you on; if you do nothing else, promise yourself you will accomplish these.

Your tasks may be modest, but just because we cannot tackle everything, it does not mean we cannot do *anything*. If possible, try to make these the first things you do.

In the evening, take a few minutes to check in with yourself and keep account. Write a couple of sentences reflecting on how things have gone. If you did not do what you intended, explore this. A journal is a place to name, not shame, so put aside self-criticism and write as an objective, compassionate friend.

You may feel you are starting small, but persistence matters more than size in 'slaying the giant'. This is an exercise to repeat daily. You could select the same stone(s) each time, rebuilding a way forward, bit by bit. As is well said, 'keep it simple, keep it real and keep it up', and you will find not only this, but other areas fall into place.

> Turn the circle into a spiral staircase

Trio of Lists

T S Eliot's poem *Ash Wednesday* uses the image of the spiral staircase to illuminate the windings of a spiritual journey. Sometimes we feel we are going round in circles, re-tracing old ground in deepening ruts. Yet, we are not the same as when we started out. As we turn and turn again, we bring with us growing knowledge and experience. We may be tracking a familiar path, but we are on a different level.

Even relapsing can contain valuable lessons, as we look back and reflect on what brought us to this point. As we seek to redirect our path, there may be things to bring with us, as well as those to leave behind; our experience may suggest some new approaches for the way ahead.

Set up three columns in your journal, to write three lists:

List 1: Those things you wish to leave behind. These may be habits, practices, routines, relationships, places, etc...

List 2: Those things you want to carry forward. This may include anything that feels important, even if it has become a bit clouded over. What has worked well for you previously? What have you done — or not done — that has been sustaining?

List 3: Those things you want to start. List 1 may be useful here, as you perhaps look for some creative alternatives for what you intend to discard.

Now re-read and review your lists, writing a few reflective sentences on what you notice, particularly about the relationship between them.

Choose some items to write about in more detail. You may want to write about an item from List 1, to underline why you no longer wish it to be a part of your life and to strengthen your resolve in letting it go. You may want to affirm and celebrate an item on List 2, as an encouragement for where you have done well. You may want to map out in a bit more detail the specifics of how you will implement something on List 3.

You could revisit this exercise after a period of time, to look at how things are going for you and to do a bit more resetting where needed.

Poetry Exploration

> Deepen understanding of your choices

'I drew a line…'

I drew a line
this far, and no further,
never will I go further than this.

When I went further,
I drew a new line,
and then another line.

The sun was shining
and everywhere I saw people,
hurried and serious,
and everyone was drawing a line,
everyone went further.

Toon Tellegen

This poem (translated from its original Dutch by Judith Wilkinson) identifies the slippage between setting an intention and following through on a commitment. In the second stanza, the Speaker is unfazed at having crossed their own line, and in the third stanza observes that they are not alone.

Good boundaries help us to preserve energy, focus attention, protect ourselves, and enable us to flourish. What lines have you drawn that worked for you in these ways?

Write the silent space between the poem's stanzas by describing a time when you drew a line across an aspect of your life that you intended, but failed, to honour. Explore, objectively and without self-blame, what led to the crossing of that line. How did you respond to your own line-crossing and where did it leave you?

Now, write in the space after the poem has ended about how you respond to everyone drawing a line and going further. Are you consoled and validated? Or resigned and dispirited? What does it mean to you that the people are 'hurried and serious'?

Alternatively, you could explore this issue in a sequenced free-write:

Write for five minutes about a time when you failed to follow through an intention, exploring what this was about for you. After five minutes, draw a line across your page underneath your writing.

Re-read what you have written and pick out a word, phrase or sentence that catches your attention. Copy this as a heading for five minutes' further writing, to go further, dig deeper and explore things more fully. Repeat this process for the final time.

As you re-read your third piece, reflect on where this succession of free-writes beyond the lines has taken you, and what has emerged.

> Find some anchorage for a reset

The Hole

The hole felt embarrassed, exposed,
too open to the elements, so
it started collecting things to fill itself in.

It began with tears, tears of laughter
tears of sorrow, tears of mourning
tears of despair, but they all drained away.

It then moved onto songs, the songs of
blackbirds, robins, the cuckoo, the crow
but they flew away when cats appeared.

It changed tack, tried poems, polemics, speeches
even took up photography, web design.
Nothing worked. It remained empty. A hole.

In desperation it asked its friend, the oak,
How do you manage to be so fulfilled?
The oak smiled. *Roots, put down some roots.*

Keith Lander

This poem explores how all our striving cannot answer our longings when our efforts are misdirected; we need to turn our attention to another area altogether. *The Hole*'s Speaker resonates with the experience of many who struggle with feelings of emptiness and vulnerability, whose immediate instinct is to address the lack by finding something to fill this intolerable space.

The Speaker pours an overwhelm of emotions into the hole, expressed in tears of both grief and joy. Next comes the music of birdsong. Finally, the hole tries to fill itself with a plethora of creative activity. Yet nothing hits the spot...

Emotion, nature, the arts, creative activities and interests: do you turn to any of these to fill your own empty times? Are there things you would add? What do you tend to collect, to smother internal discomfort?

These things are good in themselves, yet there are gaps in us they cannot address. But as so often in life, the Speaker's response is simply to keep trying to fill the same hole with something else.

The answer is not increasingly futile efforts, but a change of direction. Exhausted, the Hole becomes willing to ask for another way. The steadfast oak has the answer: roots. Roots hold us steady in all weathers, even as they draw nourishment from the soil. Where do your roots lie? It may be in a network of family or community, values, the practice of a faith, your life's rhythms and routines. Write about what steadies and holds you firm amidst change and unpredictability. Reflect on how you can stay connected to these roots.

> Find self-compassion and forgiveness

People Like Us

There are more like us. All over the world
There are confused people, who can't remember
The name of their dog when they wake up, and people
Who love God but can't remember where

He was when they went to sleep. It's
All right. The world cleanses itself this way.
A wrong number occurs to you in the middle
Of the night, you dial it, it rings just in time

To save the house. And the second-story man
Gets the wrong address, where the insomniac lives,
And he's lonely, and they talk, and the thief
Goes back to college. Even in graduate school,

You can wander into the wrong classroom,
And hear great poems lovingly spoken
By the wrong professor. And you find your soul,
And greatness has a defender, and even in death you're safe

Robert Bly

We can be idealistic about our capabilities and overly intense about getting everything right. This poem reminds us that to be human is to be imperfect. Yet, this does not always spell trouble. 'Wrong' is a word repeated in the poem, but it is not the last one. Sometimes beautiful, if unintended, consequences emerge through our very frailty.

Confusion, forgetfulness, mistakes, misremembering, errors made through inattention — all feature among the poem's six examples of a human shortcoming with a serendipitous outcome. They can surface when we are especially under pressure.

Do you identify with any of these in particular? How does the poem's take on them make you feel? Can you recall a time in your life when some unexpected and seemingly unrelated good emerged from an unplanned action, an embarrassing moment or mistake?

Write about such a time. If there are several, you could, perhaps, combine them into a list poem in the spirit of Robert Bly's poem.

As you think about recovering momentum on your onward path, can you relax a bit more? This poem can bring consolation at times when frailty and failure bring fear of being on the brink of disaster. It reminds us that we may actually be on the brink of something good.

When you find yourself…	**Writing may help you to…**
• Angry at unfairness, comparing with others	• Re-claim your own unique journey
• Overwhelmed by a setback	• Identify priorities and recover momentum
• Feeling you are re-tracking old ground	• Turn the circle into a spiral staircase
• With old reactions surfacing	• Deepen understanding of your choices
• With best efforts exhausted	• Find some anchorage for a reset
• Angry at self for not moving on	• Find self-compassion and forgiveness

References

Reacting

10 James Pennebaker has written extensively about the therapeutic value of writing. The experiment with the redundant engineers can be found Chapter 2 of *Opening Up by Writing It Down*, James W Pennebaker and Joshua M Smyth (The Guilford Pres 2016).
11 Based in Sweden, Emilie Dittmer teaches and writes about therapeutic writing. See emeliehdittmer.com.

Resisting

25 Find out more about Joseph Campbell's wide-ranging work at the Joseph Campbell Foundation www.jcf.org.
27 Visit www.meganchayes.com for Megan Hayes' work and her Joyful School of Writing.
30 *Time to Think*, Nancy Kline, (Ward Lock 1999) is about cultivating productive thinking through effective listening, mainly in an organisational context.

Reckoning

42 From East Coker, one of Four Quartets, T S Eliot.
42 *Obliquity*, John Kay, (Profile Books 2011)

Re-orientating

58 Viktor Frankl's *Man's Search for Meaning* was first published in 1946. By the time he died in 1997, it had sold 10 million copies and been translated into 24 languages. Frankl's unique psychotherapeutic method, logotherapy, posits 'the will to meaning' as the basic motivation of human life.
60 *H is for Hawk*, Helen MacDonald (Vintage 2015): a memoir about grieving a father alongside training a falcon.
61 Shut Up and Write at www.shutupandwrite.com; The Writers' Hour at www.writershour.com.
62 Amy's story has moved on. She writes: 'After three heartbreaking years of treatments and losses we decided to take a break and focus on our relationship, so we planned our wedding. Shortly after we got married I found out I was pregnant with our daughter. We couldn't believe it had happened naturally after all we had been through. Having three girls is something I am thankful for every single day, although now I'm happier I'm not writing as much poetry!'
66 Those familiar with the Myers-Briggs Personality Type Model will recognise these writing modes' correspondence with the four Myers-Briggs Functions of Sensing, Intuition, Thinking and Feeling.

Resourcing

74 The charity Maggie's offers wide-ranging support for those affected by cancer at its UK and International centres. Its founder, Maggie Keswick Jencks, intended that such support would help cancer patients 'not to lose the joy of living in the fear of dying.'

75 From *Resurrection Year: Turning Broken Dreams into New Beginnings* Sheridan Voysey (Thomas Nelson 2013). Memoir of a journey of faith through the challenge of infertility.

76 Vrjje University's research findings were published in The International Journal of Environmental Research and Public Health in 2015. See www.pmc.ncbi.nlm.nih.gov/articles/PMC4690962/.

77 *Love, Medicine and Miracles* Bernie Seigel (Rider 1999) explores common factors of positive outcomes in cancer patients.

Re-energising

90 The Radio 4 Programme was *Pearl: Two Fathers, Two Daughters*, which presented extracts from an interview with Gerry McCann alongside poet Simon Armitage's dramatisation of Pearl — a medieval poem recounting a father's grief at the loss of his young daughter.

91 *Finding Meaning: The Sixth Stage of Grief* David Kessler (Blackstone Publishing 2019).

95 The Countess of Chester Hospital, Chester.

104 See Matthew 6:28-30 at biblegateway.com.

Resolving

106 More to Life (MTL) is an initiative of Fertility Network UK, with further information at www.fertilitynetworkuk.org/life-without-children/.

107 *Revelations of Divine Love* by Julian of Norwich (1342-c.1416) is widely acknowledged as a spiritual classic and thought to be the earliest surviving English work attributed to a woman.

107 *Ambiguous Loss: Learning to Live with Unresolved Grief*, Pauline Boss (Harvard University Press 1999). See also www.ambiguousloss.com.

111 *Tales From The Rainbow Nation*, Linda Cosgriff (Seven Arches Publishing 2024) mixes poetry and prose covering the author's time in South Africa.

114 *At a Journal Workshop: The Basic Text and Guide for Using the Intensive Journal*, Ira Progoff (Dialogue House Library 1975). See also www.ntensivejournal.org.

116 *Writing the Mind Alive*, Linda Trichter Metcalf (Random House 2002). See also the Proprioceptive Writing Center at www.pwriting.org.

120 See Anthony Wilson's extensive collection of Lifesaving Poems at anthonywilsonpoetry.com.

Reconstituting

124 See www.roadpeace.org.
124 From Little Gidding, one of Four Quartets, T S Eliot.
124 *At the Will of the Body*, Arthur W Frank (Mariner Books 2002)

Relapsing

140 Ash Wednesday (particularly Part III), T S Eliot
145 See 1 Samuel 17 for the full story of David and Goliath at biblegateway.com.

Permissions

Pauline Bell "Growth." Used with the poet's permission.

Robert Bly "People like us" from *Morning Poems*. Copyright © 1997 by Robert Bly. Reprinted with permission of George Borchardt, Inc on behalf of the Estate of Robert Bly. All rights reserved.

Judy Brown "Trough" from *The Sea Accepts All Rivers and Other Poems*, Trafford Publishing.Copyright © 2016 Judy Brown. Reprinted with permission of the poet.

Maura Dooley "The Gift" from *The Silvering*, Bloodaxe Books, 2016. Reproduced with permission of Bloodaxe Books www.bloodaxebooks.com @bloodaxebooks (twitter/facebook) #bloodaxebooks

Alistair Elliot "A Northern Morning" from *Staying Alive*, Bloodaxe Books, 2002. Reprinted with permission from the Alastair Elliot Estate.

Louise Gluck "The Wild Iris" from "*The Wild Iris*" (paperback). Reprinted with the permission of Carcanet Press Ltd, University of Manchester, Oxford Road M13 9PP.

Sharron Green "The Me Before". Used with the poet's permission.

Olav H Hauge "Don't give me the whole truth," Tr. Robin Fulton, from *Leaf Huts and Snow-houses: Selected Poems* (paperback). Reprinted with the permission of Carcanet Press Ltd, University of Manchester, Oxford Road M13 9PP.

Helen Hill "All Weathers", written for Carers' Trust. Used with the poet's permission.

Keith Lander "The Hole". Used with the poet's permission.

Dorianne Laux "For the Sake of Strangers" from *What We Carry* BOA Editions Ltd, 1994, © Dorianne Laux. Reprinted with the poet's permission.

Imelda Maguire "Lost and Found" from *Shout If You Want Me To Sing*, Summer Palace Press, 2004. Reprinted with the poet's permission.

Czesław Milosz "Gift" from *New and Collected Poems 1931-2001*, Penguin Random House UK. Permission to reprint sought from Penguin Random Press.

Esther Morgan "This Morning" from *Grace*, Bloodaxe Books, 2011. Reproduced with permission of Bloodaxe Books www.bloodaxebooks.com @bloodaxebooks (twitter/facebook) #bloodaxebooks

Naomi Shihab Nye " The Art of Disappearing" from *Words under the Words: Selected Poems from Naomi Shihab Nye*. Copyright © 1980 by Naomi Shihab Nye. Reprinted with permission of Far Corner Books.

Francesca Pridham "Brooklyn Bridge." Used with the poet's permission.

Jan Richardson "Blessing in the Chaos" from *The Cure for Sorrow: A Book of Blessings in a Time of Grief,* Wanton Gospeller Press 2020. © Jan Richardson, janrichardson.com. Reprinted with the poet's permission.

Excerpt from Rebecca del Rio, "Prescription for the Disillusioned".

Andrew Rudd "Resistance" from *The Quiet Path: Contemplative Practices for Daily Life.* Canterbury Press, 2024. © Andrew Rudd 2024. Reprinted with the poet's permission.

Sarah Salway "You Do Not Need Another Self-Help Book" from *You Do Not Need Another Self-Help Book*, Pindrop Press, 2012. Reprinted with the poet's permission.

Diane Sanders "Wayfarer" from *I am Nature: Environmental Poetry* (Veneficia Publications 2025). Reprinted with the poet's permission.

Anne-Marie Smith "Writing to myself." Used with the poet's permission.

William Stafford "Ask Me" and "Things I Learned Last Week" from *Ask Me: 1000 Essential Poems.* Copyright © 2014 by the Estate of William Stafford. Reprinted with the permission of the The Permissions Company, LLC on behalf of Graywolf Press, Minneapolis, Minnesota, USA graywolfpress.org

Toon Tellegen "I drew a line" Tr. Judith Wilkinson from *Under a Giant Sky* Shoestring Press, 2019. Reprinted with the permission of the publisher.

Rosemerry Wahtola Trommer "Perhaps it Would Eventually Erode" and "The Way it Is" from *Naked for Tea.* Able Muse Press 2018. Reprinted with the poet's permission.

Lynn Ungar "Camas Lilies"; Copyright © 1995 by Lynn Ungar. First published in *Blessing the Bread*, Skinner House Books, 1996. "On the Other Side", copyright © Lynn Ungar, published in These Days: Poetry of the Pandemic Age, 2020.

Kyell Walfridsson "Restricted Living" Tr. Tommy Carlson from the journal Pietisten: *A Herald of Awakening and Spiritual Edification*; Pietisten, Inc., Winter 1999; www.pietisten.org.

Mary Woodward "Risotto" from *The White Valentine*, Worple Press, 2014. Reprinted with the publisher's permission.